THE POWER OF A HEALED WOMAN

Healing Grace: The Power of a Healed Woman

Genea' Waller

Published by Genea' Waller, 2024.

While every precaution has been taken in the preparation of this book, the publisher assumes no responsibility for errors or omissions, or for damages resulting from the use of the information contained herein.

HEALING GRACE: THE POWER OF A HEALED WOMAN

First edition. March 1, 2024.

ISBN: 979-8224307074

Written by Genea' Waller.

Table of Contents

Dedication

To My Dearest Mother,

This book is dedicated to you, the woman who has shaped my life in more ways than words can express. From the moment I entered this world, you have been my guiding light, my source of strength, and my greatest inspiration.

You have loved me with a love that knows no bounds, nurturing me, supporting me, and cheering me on every step of the way. Your unwavering faith, resilience, and grace have been a beacon of hope in the darkest of times, showing me what it means to trust in God's goodness and sovereignty.

You have taught me the power of kindness, compassion, and forgiveness, leading by example with a heart that is always ready to forgive and love unconditionally. Your selflessness and generosity know no limits, as you give of yourself freely to others, making the world a brighter and more beautiful place.

As I embark on this journey of writing, I carry with me the lessons, values, and memories that you have instilled in me. Your love and wisdom continue to guide me, shaping the words that flow from my heart onto these pages.

Thank you, Mom, for being my rock, my confidante, and my greatest cheerleader. Your love has been a constant source of strength and inspiration, and I am forever grateful for the gift of your presence in my life.

With all my love and admiration,

Genea'

Healing Grace

A Christian Guide for Women to Find Wholeness in Christ

by Genea' Waller

Healing Grace: A Christian Guide for Women to Find Wholeness in Christ

8

TABLE OF CONTENTS

Chapter 1: Surrendering to God's Healing Power

Introduction

- Embracing the journey of healing and restoration through faith.

Embracing the journey of healing and restoration through faith can be a powerful and transformative experience for many individuals. Faith in God can provide a sense of comfort, hope, and strength during challenging times. By leaning on God, individuals can find solace in knowing that they are not alone and that there is a greater purpose to their struggles.

Throughout the journey of healing and restoration, faith can serve as a guiding light, helping individuals navigate the ups and downs of life with resilience and grace. It can instill a sense of peace and acceptance, allowing individuals to let go of past hurts and resentments, and move forward towards a brighter future. By cultivating a deep sense of faith in God, individuals can find the courage to confront their, and emerge stronger and more whole than ever before.

Ultimately, embracing the journey of healing and restoration through faith in God to deliver you from all pain, trauma, loss, burdens, brokenness, fears, doubts, and insecurities, is a personal and profound experience that can lead to inner peace, self-discovery, and spiritual growth. By opening one's heart to the possibilities that God offers everything you need through your Lord and Savior Jesus Christ, individuals can embark on a transformative path towards healing, wholeness, and a renewed sense of purpose in life.

- Setting the intention to seek God's healing grace and discover our true identity in Christ.

Setting the intention to seek God's healing grace and discover your true identity in Christ is a powerful and transformative journey that many individuals embark upon in their spiritual lives. By opening our hearts to the possibility of receiving God's healing grace, we allow ourselves to release any pain, burdens, or wounds that may be holding us back from fully experiencing His love and presence in our lives.

Through prayer, meditation on the word of God, and reflection on the teachings of Christ, we can begin to uncover and embrace our true identity as beloved children of God. This process involves letting go of false beliefs, societal expectations, and past traumas that may have clouded our understanding of who we are in God's eyes. By surrendering to God's will and trusting in His plan for our lives, we can experience a profound sense of peace, purpose, and fulfillment that comes from living in alignment with our true identity in Christ.

As we continue to walk in faith and seek God's healing grace, we are reminded that we are fearfully and wonderfully made in His image. Embracing our true identity in Christ allows us to live authentically, love unconditionally, and serve others with compassion and grace. May this intention guide you on a path of spiritual growth, self-discovery, and divine healing as you deepen your relationship with God and experience the fullness of His love and mercy in your life.

Chapter 1: Surrendering to God's Healing Power

Surrendering to God's healing power can be a powerful and transformative experience for many individuals. It involves letting go of control and trusting in God to guide you towards healing and wholeness. This surrender requires a deep sense of faith and belief that God's love and grace can bring about healing in ways that may not always be immediately apparent to us.

Through surrendering to God's healing power, you can find comfort, strength, and peace in the midst of difficult circumstances. It can provide a sense of hope and renewal, allowing individuals to release their burdens and find solace in the knowledge that they are not alone in their struggles. By relinquishing control and placing their trust in God, individuals can open themselves up to receiving the healing and restoration that they seek.

Ultimately, surrendering to God's healing power is a personal journey that can bring about profound spiritual growth and emotional healing. It is a process of letting go of fear, doubt, and uncertainty, and embracing the belief that God's love and healing presence can bring about transformation and renewal in our lives. By surrendering to God's healing power, you can experience a deep sense of peace, joy, and wholeness as you allow divine grace to work in your life.

Acknowledging Pain and Brokenness

Acknowledging pain and brokenness is a crucial step in the journey towards healing and growth. It takes courage and vulnerability to confront our own struggles and acknowledge the areas in our lives that need attention and care. By recognizing our pain and brokenness, we open the door to self-awareness and self-compassion.

Rather than ignoring or suppressing our pain, acknowledging it allows us to begin the process of understanding its root causes and working towards resolution. This acknowledgment can lead to seeking support from others, whether it be through pastors, leaders, or godly counseling, or simply talking to a trusted friend or family member who has understand of the word of God and can provide sound doctrine to help on the journey of healing. It is important to remember that everyone experiences pain and brokenness at some point in their lives, and it is a common human experience to face challenges and obstacles.

In acknowledging our pain and brokenness, we give ourselves permission to be imperfect and to embrace our vulnerabilities. This act of self-compassion can be a powerful catalyst for personal growth and transformation. It is through facing our pain with courage and honesty that we can begin to heal and move towards a place of greater peace and wholeness. Before we can embark on the journey of healing, it's essential to acknowledge the pain and brokenness we carry. In this section, we'll explore the importance of facing our hurts with honesty and vulnerability, trusting God to meet us in our brokenness and lead us to wholeness.

Reflecting on Your Journey

Take a moment to reflect on your life's journey. What painful experiences have you faced? How have they impacted you emotionally, spiritually, and relationally? Allow yourself to acknowledge the depth of your pain and the areas in which you feel broken.

Embracing Vulnerability

Embrace vulnerability as a path to healing. It's okay to admit that you're hurting and struggling. Share your feelings with God, he won't let you down. Allow yourself to be supported and loved in your vulnerability, knowing that God sees and understands your pain.

Surrendering to God's Healing Grace

Surrender your pain and brokenness to God. Release the burden of carrying it alone and invite God to enter into your woundedness. Trust that His healing grace is sufficient to mend your brokenness and restore your soul. Offer a prayer of surrender, pouring out your heart to God and inviting His healing presence into your life.

My grace is sufficient for you, for my power is made perfect in weakness. 2 Corinthians 12:9

Finding Comfort in Scripture

Find comfort and strength in the promises of Scripture. Meditate on verses that speak to God's compassion, mercy, and faithfulness. Allow His word to penetrate your heart and bring hope to your weary soul. Spend time in prayer, asking God to speak to you through His word and minister to your brokenness.

Prayer

Heavenly Father, I come before you with a heart that is broken and weary. I acknowledge the pain and brokenness I carry, and I invite you into the depths of my woundedness. Pour out your healing grace upon me, Lord, and mend the broken pieces of my heart. Give me the courage to embrace vulnerability and the strength to surrender my pain to you. Comfort me with your presence, O God, and fill me with your peace that surpasses all understanding. In Jesus' name, Amen.

Surrendering Hurt and Resentment to God

Surrendering hurt and resentment to God can be a powerful way to find peace and healing in your life. Holding onto feelings of hurt and resentment can weigh you down and prevent you from moving forward. By releasing these negative emotions to God, you can experience a sense of relief and forgiveness.

One way to surrender hurt and resentment to God is through prayer. Take the time to express your feelings honestly and openly to God, asking for help in letting go of these emotions. Trust that God is listening and that He can help you find the strength to forgive and move on.

Additionally, practicing gratitude can also help in surrendering hurt and resentment. Focus on the blessings in your life and try to shift your perspective towards positivity. By choosing to let go of negative emotions and embrace gratitude, you can create space for healing and peace to enter your heart. Trust in God's love and guidance as you navigate the journey towards forgiveness and emotional freedom.

In this section, we'll explore the transformative power of surrendering our hurt and resentment to God. Holding onto bitterness and unforgiveness only hinders our healing and blocks God's blessings in our lives. Through surrender, we open ourselves to His healing touch and experience the freedom that comes from forgiveness.

Recognizing the Weight of Hurt and Resentment

Take a moment to acknowledge the burden of hurt and resentment you've been carrying. Reflect on the ways it has affected your thoughts, emotions, and relationships. Understand that holding onto these negative emotions only keeps you trapped in a cycle of pain and bitterness.

Choosing Forgiveness

Make the conscious choice to forgive those who have hurt you. Understand that forgiveness is not excusing or condoning their actions but releasing yourself from the bondage of resentment. Ask God to help you extend grace and mercy to others as He has done for you. Forgiveness is more about you than the other person. It's the one opportunity to be selfish. Selfish to the extent of wanting and desiring to be free from an unforgiven heart.

And be kind to one another, tender-hearted, forgiving each other, just as God in Christ also has forgiven you. Ephesians 4:32

Surrendering to God's Healing Grace

Surrender your hurt and resentment to God, laying it at the foot of the cross. Trust that His grace is sufficient to heal your wounded heart and restore your peace. Surrendering doesn't mean denying your pain but allowing God to work in and through it for your good.

Praying for Healing and Restoration

Pour out your heart to God in prayer, expressing your pain, anger, and struggles. Ask Him to heal the wounds of your past and fill you with His love and forgiveness. Pray for the strength to let go of bitterness and embrace the freedom that comes from surrendering to His will.

Cultivating a Heart of Gratitude

Cultivate a heart of gratitude by focusing on God's goodness and faithfulness in your life. Count your blessings and thank God for His mercy and grace. As you shift your focus from past hurts to present blessings, you'll find joy and peace in His presence.

Prayer

Heavenly Father, I come before you with a heart heavy with hurt and resentment. I acknowledge the pain I've been carrying and the bitterness that has taken root in my heart. Lord, I choose to forgive those who have wronged me and release them into your hands. God, I ask that you release me from the spirit of heaviness and pour out the oil of gladness upon me. I surrender my hurt and resentment to you, trusting in your healing grace to restore my soul. Fill me with your peace and love, O God, and help me to walk in forgiveness and freedom. In Jesus' name, Amen.

Embracing Forgiveness and Letting Go

Embracing forgiveness and letting go are powerful acts that can bring immense peace and healing into our lives. Forgiveness is not about condoning the hurtful actions of others, but rather about releasing the negative emotions that bind us to the past. It is a gift we give ourselves, allowing us to move forward without carrying the heavy burden of resentment and anger.

Letting go is closely tied to forgiveness, as it involves releasing attachments to things, people, or situations that no longer serve us. By letting go, we create space for new opportunities, growth, and positivity to enter our lives. It requires courage and self-awareness to confront our fears and insecurities, but the rewards of inner freedom and emotional well-being are invaluable.

Together, embracing forgiveness and letting go can lead to a profound sense of liberation and transformation. By practicing these acts regularly, we cultivate a mindset of compassion, resilience, and gratitude, paving the way for greater peace, joy, and fulfillment in our journey through life.

Embracing Forgiveness and Letting Go

Forgiveness is a powerful act of liberation that frees us from the chains of resentment and bitterness. The enemy plan is to break you in hopes that you will go throughout life so broken and battered to get you to think no one loves you, no one cares, and you cannot be healed and restored. But Jesus is a healer. If He can heal physical sickness and diseases instantly, how much more can He take away all the pain and brokenness within your heart? In this section, we'll explore the transformative journey of embracing forgiveness and letting go of past hurts. Through God's grace, we can release the weight of unforgiveness and experience the healing that comes from extending mercy to others.

Understanding the Gift of Forgiveness

Take time to reflect on the meaning and significance of forgiveness. Recognize that forgiveness is not condoning or excusing the wrongdoing but choosing to release the offender from the debt they owe you. Understand that forgiveness is a gift you give yourself, allowing you to move forward in freedom and peace.

And whenever you stand praying, if you have anything against anyone, forgive him, that your Father in heaven may also forgive you your trespasses. Mark 11:25

Examining Your Heart

Examine your heart honestly and identify any areas of unforgiveness or resentment. Reflect on the specific incidents or individuals that have caused you pain. Acknowledge the emotions that arise as you confront these hurts, allowing yourself to feel and process them in God's presence.

Search me [thoroughly], O God, and know my heart; Test me and know my anxious thoughts; And see if there is any wicked or hurtful way in me, and lead me in the everlasting way. Psalm 139:23-24

Choosing to Forgive

Make the intentional choice to forgive those who have hurt you. Release them from the burden of their actions and let go of any desire for revenge or justice. Choose to extend the same grace and mercy that God has shown you, recognizing that forgiveness is an act of obedience and love. Forgiveness is a choose. It's up to you to decide what you allow to continue to harbor in your heart. It may not be your fault what happened to you, but it is your responsible to heal.

To You, O Lord, I lift up my soul. Psalm 25:1

Surrendering to God's Healing

Surrender your pain and bitterness to God, inviting His healing presence into your heart. Trust that God is faithful to heal the wounds of the past and restore what has been broken. Surrender your need for control and justice, allowing God to work His redemption in every situation.

Walking in Freedom

Embrace the freedom that comes from forgiveness. Release yourself from the prison of unforgiveness and embrace the abundant life that God has promised. Walk confidently in the knowledge that you are loved, accepted, and forgiven by your Heavenly Father. There is liberty where the Spirit of the Lord is. Let the Holy Spirit bring to your memory things of the past that the enemy is still using against you in hopes that you remain broken. Oftentimes, the enemy will have you bury the memory, but the pain still exudes from your heart. Through your words, actions, and mannerism we demonstrate daily how we truly feel about ourselves and others

How can you speak good things when you are evil (wicked)? For out of the fullness (the overflow, the (superabundance) of the heart the mouth speaks. Matthew 12:34

Prayer

Gracious God, I come before you with a heart weighed down by unforgiveness and bitterness. I acknowledge the pain that I've been holding onto and the freedom that comes from forgiveness. Help me to extend grace and mercy to those who have hurt me, just as you have shown me grace and mercy. I break agreement and covenant with the spirit of unforgiveness. Fill me with your love and peace, O Lord, and empower me to walk in forgiveness and freedom. In Jesus' name, Amen.

Opening Your Heart to Receive God's Healing Grace

Opening your heart to receive God's healing grace can be a transformative and deeply spiritual experience. It involves surrendering your worries, doubts, and fears to God, trusting that divine intervention will bring comfort and restoration to your soul. Through prayer, and reflection, you can create a sacred space within yourself where God's love and healing energy can flow freely.

To begin this journey, it's important to let go of any resistance or barriers that may be blocking the healing grace from entering your heart. This may involve forgiving yourself and others, releasing past traumas, and practicing self-love and compassion. By cultivating a sense of openness and receptivity, you create the perfect conditions for God's healing grace to work its miracles in your life. You are worthy of God's love. God loves for you is everlasting, pure, honest, and unconditional. He gave us the greatest gift when he gave us Jesus.

For God so loved the world that He gave His only begotten Son, that whoever believes in Him should not perish but have everlasting life. John 3:16

Remember that God's healing grace is boundless and unconditional, available to all who seek it with sincerity and faith. Allow yourself to be vulnerable, humble, and receptive to the blessings that come your way. Trust that God's plan for your healing is perfect, and have faith that through His grace, you will find peace, comfort, and renewal in your heart and soul.

God's healing grace is a gift freely offered to all who are willing to receive it. in this section, we'll explore the importance of opening your heart to God's healing grace, allowing His love to penetrate the deepest wounds and bring restoration to your soul.

Acknowledging Your Need for Healing

Begin by acknowledging your need for healing. Recognize that you are not meant to carry your burdens alone and that God desires to bring healing and restoration to every area of your life. Take time to reflect on the areas where you need healing the most, whether they be physical, emotional, or spiritual. Be honest with Jesus. Tell Him what you have been through. He already knows, but He's waiting on you to talk to Him about it.

Casting all your care upon Him, for He cares for you. 1 Peter 5:7

Surrendering Control to God

Surrender control of your healing journey to God. Let go of any desire to fix things on your own and trust in God's perfect timing and plan. Release any doubts or fears that may be holding you back and place your faith fully in His ability to heal and restore.

Cultivating a Heart of Faith and Expectancy

Cultivate a heart of faith and expectancy, believing that God is able and willing to heal you completely. Lean into His promises and hold onto the hope that He offers. Surround yourself with reminders of His faithfulness and provision, filling your mind with His truth.

Receiving God's Love and Forgiveness

Open your heart to receive God's love and forgiveness. Allow His grace to wash over you, cleansing you from all guilt and shame. Receive His unconditional love with gratitude and allow it to penetrate the deepest recesses of your heart, bringing healing and wholeness.

Practicing Gratitude and Praise

Practice gratitude and praise as you await God's healing touch. Give thanks for the blessings He has already bestowed upon you and praise Him for His faithfulness and goodness. Let your heart overflow with gratitude, knowing that He is faithful to fulfill His promises.

Prayer

HEALING GRACE: THE POWER OF A HEALED WOMAN

Heavenly Father, I come before you with a heart open and ready to receive your healing grace. I acknowledge my need for healing and surrender control of my journey to you. Fill me with faith and expectancy, Lord, believing that you are able to do exceedingly abundantly above all that I ask or think. Pour out your love and forgiveness upon me, O God, and bring healing and restoration to every area of my life. In Jesus' name, Amen.

Chapter 2: Discovering Your Identity in Christ

Discovering your identity in Christ is a profound and transformative journey for many individuals. It involves understanding who you are as a beloved child of God, created in His image with unique gifts, talents, calling, and assignments. Embracing your identity in Christ means recognizing that you are deeply loved, forgiven, and accepted just as you are, regardless of your past mistakes or shortcomings.

As you delve into your identity in Christ, you may uncover new aspects of yourself that align with God's plan for your life. This can bring a sense of peace, purpose, and fulfillment as you strive to live out your faith in a way that reflects your true identity. Through prayer, studying the Word, and seeking guidance from fellow believers, you can deepen your understanding of who you are in Christ and the incredible potential you have to make a positive impact in the world.

Ultimately, discovering your identity in Christ is a journey of growth, self-discovery, and spiritual transformation that can lead to a deeper relationship with God and a clearer sense of purpose in your life. By embracing your identity as a child of God, you can find strength, courage, and joy in knowing that you are valued and cherished beyond measure.

Our true identity is found in Christ alone. In this section, we'll embark on a journey of self-discovery rooted in our relationship with Him. By understanding who we are in Christ, we can live out our God-given purpose and walk confidently in His truth.

Understanding Your Value and Worth

Reflect on the truth that you are fearfully and wonderfully made in the image of God (Psalm 139:14). Recognize that your value and worth are not determined by your accomplishments or external appearance but by the fact that you are a beloved child of God.

She is more precious than rubies, and all the things you may desire cannot compare with her. Proverbs 3:15

Embracing Your Identity as a daughter of the King

Embrace your identity as a daughter of the King. As a co-heir with Christ, you are royalty in His kingdom (Romans 8:17). Allow this truth to shape how you see yourself and how you interact with the world around you.

And if children, then heirs—heirs of God and joint heirs with Christ, if indeed we suffer with Him, that we may also be glorified together. Romans 8:17

Letting Go of Labels and Lies

Release yourself from the labels and lies that the world may try to place on you. You are not defined by your past mistakes, your failures, or the opinions of others. Instead, you are defined by God's love and grace.

Discovering Your Unique Purpose

Seek God's guidance in discovering your unique purpose and calling. Spend time in prayer and reflection, asking Him to reveal the gifts, talents, and passions He has placed within you. Trust that He has a specific plan for your life and that He will equip you to fulfill it.

Walking in Confidence and Boldness

Walk in confidence and boldness as you embrace your identity in Christ. Know that you are equipped with everything you need to fulfill God's purpose for your life (2 Timothy 1:7). Step out in faith, trusting that He will guide and empower you every step of the way.

Now this is the confidence that we have in Him, that if we ask anything according to His will, He hears us. 1 John 5:14

Prayer

Heavenly Father, thank you for the incredible privilege of being called your child. I break free from the lies of the false accusation spoken over me and life from the accuser of the brethren. That is not who I am or who you called me to be. You have called me the righteousness of you, and the apple of your eye. I choose from this day forward Lord to only identify with who you say I am. Help me to fully embrace my identity in Christ and to live out the purpose you have for my life. Give me the strength to let go of labels and lies, and to walk confidently in your truth. May my life bring glory to your name, O Lord. In Jesus' name, amen.

Understanding God's Love and Purpose for You

Understanding God's love and purpose for you is a profound journey that many embark upon in their lifetime. The concept of God's love is often described as unconditional, all-encompassing, and unfailing. It is believed that God's love knows no bounds and extends to every individual, regardless of their past actions or beliefs. This love is said to provide comfort, guidance, and strength in times of need, serving as a source of hope and inspiration for many.

Many people seek to understand their purpose in life the standards set by the world, but as the children of God we live in this world but we are not of the world, so we don't go about things the way the world does. God has a unique plan for you. You have a specific role to fulfill in the world, shaped by their talents, passions, and experiences. Discovering this purpose often involves introspection, prayer, and seeking guidance from spiritual teachings. By aligning oneself with God's will, individuals may find fulfillment, peace, and a sense of meaning in their daily lives.

Ultimately, the journey to understanding God's love and purpose for you is a deeply personal and spiritual one. It requires an open heart, a willingness to listen, and a commitment to living in alignment with God's written word. Through prayer, reflection, and seeking wisdom, God will lead you and guide you. Acknowledge, that you don't know or have all the answer, but you believe and trust God to show His perfect plan and design for your life.

God's love for you is beyond measure, and His purpose for your life is filled with hope and promise. In this section, we'll delve into the depths of God's love and explore His unique purpose for you, drawing strength and encouragement from His unending grace.

Embracing God's Unconditional Love

Reflect on the depth of God's unconditional love for you. Despite your flaws and shortcomings, God's love remains constant and unwavering. Take time to meditate on scriptures that speak of His love, such as John 3:16 and Romans 8:38-39, and allow His truth to penetrate your heart.

Recognizing Your Worth in His Eyes

Recognize your worth in God's eyes. You are precious and valuable to Him, created in His image and chosen to be His beloved child. Let go of any feelings of inadequacy or unworthiness, knowing that you are deeply loved and cherished by your Heavenly Father.

But you are a chosen generation, a royal priesthood, a holy nation, His own special people, that you

may proclaim the praises of Him who called you out of darkness into His marvelous light; 1 Peter 2:9

Trusting His Perfect Timing

Trust in God's perfect timing for your life. He has a plan and purpose for you, and He knows the desires of your heart. Surrender your timeline to Him and trust that He will fulfill His promises in His perfect way and timing.

Seeking His Will Through Prayer

Seek God's will for your life through prayer and communion with Him. Spend time in His presence, listening for His still, small voice and seeking His guidance for your next steps. Be open to His leading, knowing that He desires to direct your paths and fulfill His purposes through you.

In all your ways acknowledge Him, And He shall direct your paths. Proverbs 3:6

Walking in Faith and Obedience

Walk in faith and obedience as you follow God's leading in your life. Step out in courage, trusting that He will equip you with everything you need to fulfill His purpose for you. Allow His love to be the guiding force in your decisions and actions, knowing that He works all things together for your good.

If you are willing and obedient, you shall eat the good of the land; Isaiah 1:19

Prayer

Heavenly Father, thank you for your unfailing love and the purpose you have for my life. Help me to fully embrace your love and to trust in your perfect plan for me. You said in your word that your plans are not to harm me, but to prosper me and give me a hope and a future. You are not a man that you should lie, neither are you the Son of Man that you need to repent. You make no mistake or error. You are perfect in all your ways. Give me the courage to step out in faith and obedience, knowing that you are with me every step of the way. May my life bring glory to your name, O Lord. In Jesus' name, amen.

Reflecting on Biblical Examples of God's Redemption

Throughout the Bible, we find countless stories of God's redemption and restoration. In this section, we'll explore some of these powerful examples, drawing inspiration and hope from the ways God has transformed lives and brought redemption to His people.

Examining the Story of Ruth

Reflect on the story of Ruth, a woman who experienced loss and hardship but found redemption and restoration through her unwavering faith and loyalty. Consider how God used her obedience and trust to bring about His purposes, ultimately leading to blessings beyond her wildest dreams.

Meditating on the Life of David

Meditate on the life of David, a man after God's own heart who experienced both triumph and failure. Despite his shortcomings, David found redemption through repentance and God's mercy, ultimately fulfilling his purpose as king of Israel and ancestor of Jesus Christ.

Contemplating the Conversion of Paul

Contemplate the transformation of Paul, a persecutor of Christians who became one of the greatest evangelists of all time. Consider how God's grace and power can turn even the most hardened hearts and use them for His glory.

Reflecting on the Prodigal Son

Reflect on the parable of the prodigal son, a powerful illustration of God's unconditional love and forgiveness. Consider how God welcomes us back into His arms with open arms, no matter how far we may have strayed.

Applying Lessons to Your Own Life

Apply the lessons learned from these biblical examples to your own life. Consider how God's redemption and restoration are at work in your own story, even in the midst of pain and struggle. Trust that God is able to redeem even the most broken areas of your life and use them for His glory.

Prayer

Heavenly Father, thank you for the countless examples of redemption and restoration found throughout your Word.

Help me to draw strength and hope from these stories, knowing that you are able to redeem even the most broken areas of my life. Your words says you will redeem the time because the days are evil. Set me free from generation patterns, blockages, hinderes, lies, sabotage, and partitions that are cause redemption and restoration to not take place in my life. Give me faith to trust in your plan and purpose for me, knowing that you are always at work for my good. In Jesus' name, amen.

Affirming Your Worth and Value as a daughter of God

Affirming your worth and value as a daughter of God is a powerful and uplifting practice that can bring immense peace and strength to your life. Recognizing that you are a cherished child of a God Almighty can help you navigate challenges with grace and confidence. Remembering that you are loved unconditionally can provide comfort during times of doubt or difficulty.

As a daughter of God, you possess inherent value and worth that is not dependent on external measures of success or approval. Embracing your divine identity can inspire you to treat yourself and others with kindness, compassion, and respect. By acknowledging your worthiness as a child of God, you can cultivate a sense of purpose and fulfillment that transcends worldly standards.

In moments of self-doubt or struggle, take time to reflect on your divine nature and the limitless potential that resides within you. Trust in the love and guidance of God, knowing that you are never alone on your journey. Affirm your worth as a daughter of God by embracing your unique gifts, talents, and strengths, and by sharing them with the world in a spirit of love and service.

In this section, we will delve into the profound truth of your worth and value as a beloved daughter of God. By embracing this foundational truth, you can live with confidence and assurance, knowing that you are deeply loved and cherished by your Heavenly Father.

Embracing Your Identity in Christ

Reflect on your identity in Christ as a daughter of God. Recognize that your worth and value are not based on your accomplishments, appearance, or the opinions of others, but on your status as a cherished child of the King of Kings.

Meditating on Scripture

Meditate on scriptures that affirm your worth and value in God's eyes. Allow these truths to penetrate your heart and renew your mind. Some verses to consider include Psalm 139:14, Ephesians 2:10, and 1 Peter 2:9.

Rejecting Lies of Inadequacy

Reject any lies of inadequacy or unworthiness that may have taken root in your mind. Remind yourself that you are fearfully and wonderfully made by a loving Creator, and that your value is inherent and unchanging.

Practicing Self-Compassion

Practice self-compassion and self-care as you embrace your worth as a daughter of God. Treat yourself with the same love, kindness, and grace that God extends to you. Take time to nurture your physical, emotional, and spiritual well-being.

Walking in Confidence

Walk in confidence as you affirm your worth and value in Christ. Let go of comparison and perfectionism, knowing that you are accepted and loved just as you are. Embrace your unique gifts, talents, and calling, and use them to glorify God and bless others. You don't need to be perfect, nor does God expect you to be. This why we need Jesus. He is perfect and through His Spirit we are being perfected by God's grace in mercy. We are being made into His image. Christ's image.

Prayer

Heavenly Father, thank you for loving me unconditionally and for calling me your beloved daughter. Help me to embrace my worth and value in Christ, knowing that I am fearfully and wonderfully made in your image. Thank you for showing me that I am worthy of you. Thank you, Lord, that your perfect love cast out all fear. Give me the strength to reject lies of inadequacy and to walk in confidence as your cherished child. In Jesus' name, amen.

Embracing Your Unique Gifts and Talents

Embracing your unique gifts and talents is a powerful way to unlock your full potential and live a fulfilling life. Each person possesses a set of strengths and abilities that make them special and valuable. By recognizing and embracing these gifts, you can cultivate a sense of purpose and direction in your life.

One key aspect of embracing your unique gifts is self-awareness. Take the time to reflect on what you are naturally good at and what brings you joy. Whether it's a talent for art, writing, problem-solving, or connecting with others, acknowledging and nurturing these skills can lead to personal growth and success.

Moreover, don't be afraid to share your gifts with the world. By expressing yourself authentically and using your talents to make a positive impact, you can inspire others and create meaningful connections. Remember, the world benefits when individuals embrace their uniqueness and contribute their gifts for the will and purpose of God. So, embrace your gifts, celebrate your uniqueness, and let your light shine bright!

**Let your light so shine before men, that they may see your good works and glorify your Father in heaven.
Matthew 5:16**

Chapter 3: Renewing Your Mind with Biblical Truth

In this section, we will explore the transformative power of renewing your mind with biblical truth. By aligning your thoughts with God's Word, you can experience freedom from negative thinking patterns and live in the fullness of His truth and promises.

Recognizing Negative Thought Patterns

Take time to recognize any negative thought patterns that may be influencing your mindset. These can include thoughts of fear, doubt, insecurity, or unworthiness. When intrusive thoughts come, and the will. You have to rebuke the thoughts. This can only be done through your words. You have been authority and power through your words. Your tongue is weapon and the enemy is afraid of the power that you possess. I use a method I learn. REBUKE AND REPLACE. REBUKE. what the enemy is saying, and REPLACE it with the word of God. This means you will need to familiarize yourself with scripture. The word is power, but it must decree and declare. This is why the enemy will always get you to become silent, and deceive it that the thoughts will go away. But they will progress. We will talk more about that later on.

Casting down arguments and every high thing that exalts itself against the knowledge of God, bringing every thought into

captivity to the obedience of Christ. 2 Corinthians 10:5

Identifying Biblical Truths

Identify biblical truths that counteract these negative thought patterns. Search the scriptures for verses that speak to God's love, faithfulness, and promises for your life. Meditate on these truths and allow them to permeate your mind and heart. Write out faith confession using scriptures. Speak them over yourself daily! Sometimes multiple times a day.

Memorizing Scripture

Commit scripture to memory as a powerful tool for renewing your mind. Choose key verses that address areas of struggle or insecurity in your life and repeat them regularly. Allow God's Word to become a constant presence in your thoughts and conversations. Jesus is a present help. He will comfort and deliver you from anything you are facing. Nothing is too big or greater than our God.

God is our refuge and strength, A very present help in trouble. Psalms 46:1

Challenging Negative Thoughts

Challenge negative thoughts with biblical truth whenever they arise. When you notice yourself entertaining thoughts that are contrary to God's Word, intentionally replace them with God's word, His truth, and promises. Refuse to dwell on lies that undermine your identity and worth in Christ. When Jesus was in the wilderness being tempted by the enemy, He would only combat what the enemy was saying with the word of God by saying. IT IS WRITTEN. Jesus knew that the enemy knew the word too, so He hand to stand on the proven word of God, and not any lies or deception the enemy was speaking. The enemy came to tempt Jesus. Once, Jesus proclaimed the word of God, the enemy left him.

Cultivating a Positive Mindset

Cultivate a positive mindset by saturating your mind with God's Word. Surround yourself with uplifting resources such as Christian books, podcasts, and music that reinforce biblical truth. Stay connected to a community of believers who can encourage and support you in your journey of renewing your mind.

Walking in Freedom

Walk in the freedom that comes from renewing your mind with biblical truth. As you align your thoughts with God's Word, you will experience a transformation in your attitudes, beliefs, and behaviors. Trust in the power of God's truth to renew, restore, and refresh your mind daily.

Now the Lord is the Spirit; and where the Spirit of the Lord is, there is liberty.
2 Corinthians 3:17

Prayer

Heavenly Father, thank you for the power of your Word to renew and transform my mind. Help me to identify and challenge negative thought patterns with biblical truth. I cast down every imagination, thought, every high thing, unclean spirit, and I arrest it and bring it into the obedience of Jesus Christ. Fill me with your Spirit and empower me to walk in the freedom and victory that comes from aligning my thoughts with your Word. In Jesus' name, amen.

Challenging Negative Thought Patterns

Challenging negative thought patterns is a crucial step towards improving mental well-being and overall happiness. Negative thoughts can often spiral out of control, leading to increased stress, anxiety, and even depression. One effective technique to challenge these patterns is to practice cognitive restructuring. This involves identifying negative thoughts, questioning their validity, and replacing them with more balanced and realistic ones. By challenging the accuracy and helpfulness of negative thoughts, you can begin to reframe your perspective and cultivate a more positive mindset.

Another helpful strategy is mindfulness, which involves staying present in the moment and observing your thoughts and the intrusive thoughts of the enemy. This can help you become more aware of demonic thought patterns of the enemy as they arise, allowing you to choose whether to engage with them or let them pass by. Everything you think isn't from you. The plants lies that you can believe that is your own because he is deceptive. The Bible refers to him as the Prince and Power of the Air.

Negative thought patterns can have a significant impact on our mental and emotional well-being, hindering us from experiencing the abundant life God intends for us. In this section, we will explore strategies for identifying and challenging these harmful patterns, replacing them with thoughts that align with God's truth and promises.

Awareness of Negative Thoughts

Become aware of negative thoughts as they arise throughout your day. Notice the themes and patterns that recur, such as self-doubt, fear of failure, or feelings of inadequacy. Acknowledge that these thoughts are not aligned with God's truth for your life.

Questioning the Validity of Demonic Thoughts

Question the validity of demonic thoughts by challenging the accuracy and relevance. Ask yourself if there is evidence to support these thoughts or if they are based on assumptions or past experiences. Are these lies, false accusations, or condemnation from the enemy? Is this what God says about me? Consider alternative perspectives that align with God's truth and love for you.

Reframing Negative Thoughts with Truth

Reframe negative thoughts with biblical truth and positive affirmations. Replace lies with promises from God's Word that affirm your worth, identity, and purpose. For example, if you struggle with feelings of unworthiness, remind yourself that you are fearfully and wonderfully made in God's image (Psalm 139:14).

Practicing Gratitude and Perspective Shifts

Practice gratitude and shift your perspective toward the positive aspects of your life. Cultivate a habit of gratitude by intentionally focusing on blessings, even in the midst of challenges. Redirect your thoughts toward God's faithfulness and provision, recognizing His goodness in every circumstance.

Seeking Support and Accountability

Seek support and accountability from trusted friends, family members, or mentors who can help you challenge negative thought patterns. Share your struggles openly and invite others to pray for and encourage you in your journey toward mental and emotional wholeness.

Committing to Daily Renewal

Commit to daily renewal of your mind through prayer, meditation on Scripture, and intentional reflection. Take time each day to align your thoughts with God's truth and invite His presence to transform your mind and heart. Trust in His promise to renew you day by day (2 Corinthians 4:16).

Prayer

Heavenly Father, I confess that I often struggle with negative thought patterns that hinder me from experiencing the abundant life you have promised. I give you full permission Holy Spirit to silence the voice of any and all unclean and tormenting spirits. Help me to become aware of these thoughts and to challenge them with your truth and love. Renew my mind and transform my thinking so that I may walk in freedom and joy. In Jesus' name, amen.

Meditating on Scripture for Healing and Renewal

Meditating on Bible scriptures can be a powerful way to find healing and renewal in your life. The Bible is filled with verses that offer comfort, hope, and strength during challenging times. One such verse is Jeremiah 17:14, which says, "Heal me, O Lord, and I shall be healed; save me, and I shall be saved, for you are my praise." This verse reminds us that God is our ultimate healer and source of salvation.

Another verse that can bring healing and renewal is Isaiah 40:31, "But those who hope in the Lord will renew their strength. They will soar on wings like eagles; they will run and not grow weary; they will walk and not be faint." This verse encourages us to trust in God and find our strength in Him, knowing that He will renew us when we are feeling weary or tired.

By meditating on these and other Bible scriptures, you can find peace, comfort, and healing for your mind, body, and spirit. Take time each day to reflect on these verses, pray for healing, and renew your faith in God's love and power to restore and uplift you.

Replacing Lies with God's Truths

Replacing lies with God's truths involves identifying and challenging the negative beliefs or misconceptions we hold about ourselves, others, and the world around us, and replacing them with the positive, affirming truths found in the teachings of God.

One key aspect of replacing lies with God's truths is to spend time in prayer and reflection, seeking guidance and wisdom from God to help us discern the lies we have believed and the truths we need to embrace. Reading and studying the Bible can also be a powerful tool in uncovering God's truths and applying them to our lives.

It's important to surround ourselves with a supportive community of believers who can help us recognize and challenge the lies we may be holding onto, and who can speak God's truths into our lives. By consistently seeking God's truths and aligning our thoughts and beliefs with His word, we can experience transformation and renewal in our minds and hearts.

In this section, we will explore the process of identifying and replacing lies with God's truths. By recognizing the lies that hinder us and replacing them with the truth of God's Word, we can experience freedom, healing, and transformation in our lives.

Identifying Lies

Begin by identifying the lies that you have been believing about yourself, God, and your circumstances. These lies may manifest as negative self-talk, distorted perceptions, or feelings of shame and unworthiness. Take time to reflect on the thoughts and beliefs that hold you captive.

Searching Scripture for Truth

Search Scripture for truths that counteract the lies you have identified. Look for verses that affirm your identity in Christ, God's love and faithfulness, and His promises for your life. Allow God's Word to challenge and confront the lies that have taken root in your mind and heart.

Memorizing Key Verses

Memorize key verses of Scripture that speak directly to the lies you are struggling with. Commit these verses to memory so that they are readily available to counteract negative thoughts and beliefs. Use them as a weapon against the enemy's lies and as a source of encouragement and strength.

Meditating on Truth Daily

Make a daily practice of meditating on God's truths and applying them to your life. Set aside time each day to reflect on the verses you have memorized, allowing them to penetrate your heart and mind.

Reject the lies that bombard you and replace them with the truth of God's Word.

Speaking Truth Over Yourself

Speak God's truth over yourself daily, affirming who you are in Christ and declaring His promises over your life. Use affirmations based on Scripture to combat negative self-talk and build up your faith and confidence. Let the truth of God's Word shape your thoughts, words, and actions.

Seeking Accountability and Support

Seek accountability and support from trusted friends, family members, or mentors who can help you identify and replace lies with God's truths. Share your struggles openly and invite others to speak truth into your life. Surround yourself with a community of believers who will encourage and uplift you in your journey of transformation.

Declaring Affirmations of Faith and Identity

Declaring affirmations of faith and identity can be a powerful practice that helps you to reaffirm your beliefs, values, and sense of self. Affirmations are positive statements that can be repeated to yourself regularly to instill confidence, motivation, and a sense of purpose. When it comes to faith, affirmations can help you strengthen your spiritual connection, deepen your beliefs, and stay grounded in times of uncertainty. By declaring affirmations of faith, you are reminding yourself of what you hold dear and what guides you in life.

Similarly, affirmations of identity can help you embrace who you are, celebrate your uniqueness, and build self-acceptance. By affirming your identity, you are acknowledging your strengths, values, and experiences that shape you as an individual. This practice can boost your self-esteem, foster self-love, and empower you to navigate challenges with resilience. Whether you are declaring affirmations of faith, identity, or both, remember to personalize your statements to reflect your beliefs and values authentically. Embrace the power of positive affirmations to uplift your spirit and nurture a strong sense of self.

Prayer

Heavenly Father, thank you for the truth of your Word, which sets us free from the lies that bind us. Help me to identify and replace the lies I have been believing with your truths. Lord real your truth to me in your word and with the help of the Holy Spirit, who is my teacher and friend. Renew my mind and transform my heart so that I may walk in the fullness of your freedom and grace. In Jesus' name, amen.

Chapter 4: Cultivating a Life of Prayer and Worship

Cultivating a life of prayer and worship can bring about a profound sense of peace, connection, and spiritual fulfillment. Prayer is a way to communicate with God, express gratitude, seek guidance, and find solace during challenging times. To cultivate a consistent prayer practice, it can be helpful to set aside dedicated time each day for reflection.

God is Spirit, and those who worship Him in spirit and truth. John 4:24

In this section, we will explore the profound impact of cultivating a life characterized by prayer and worship. As women prioritize communion with God and surrender their hearts in worship, they experience deep intimacy with Him, transformation in their innermost being, and empowerment to live out their faith boldly.

Understanding the Importance of Prayer and Worship

Recognize the significance of prayer and worship in the life of a believer. Prayer is the avenue through which we communicate with God, pouring out our hearts, seeking His guidance, and interceding for others. Worship is our response to God's greatness, expressing adoration, gratitude, and surrender.

Establishing a Daily Devotional Practice

Establish a daily devotional practice that includes both prayer and worship. Set aside dedicated time each day to seek God's presence, whether it's in the morning, during a lunch break, or before bed. Create a sacred space where you can retreat from distractions and focus your heart and mind on Him.

Deepening Your Prayer Life

Deepen your prayer life by incorporating different forms of prayer, such as intercessory prayer, thanksgiving, and confession.

Engaging in Authentic Worship

Engage in authentic worship that flows from a heart surrendered to God. Worship Him in spirit and truth, offering your whole self as a living sacrifice of praise. Express your worship through music, song, dance, or creative expression, allowing the Holy Spirit to lead you into deeper intimacy with God.

Cultivating a Lifestyle of Prayer and Worship

Cultivate a lifestyle of prayer and worship that permeates every aspect of your life. Invite God into your daily routines, inviting Him to be present in your work, relationships, and leisure activities. Seek to glorify Him in all that you do, living as a reflection of His love and grace to the world around you.

Nurturing Community and Accountability

Nurture community and accountability in your prayer and worship journey by connecting with other believers who share your passion for God. Join a small group, prayer circle, or worship team where you can pray, worship, and grow together in faith. Hold one another accountable in your commitment to cultivating a life of prayer and worship.

Prayer

Heavenly Father, thank you for the privilege of prayer and worship, through which we can draw near to you and experience your presence in our lives. Help me to cultivate a life characterized by intimate communion with you, deepening my prayer life and engaging in authentic worship. May my life be a pleasing offering of praise to you. In Jesus' name, amen.

4.1 Establishing a Daily Prayer Routine

Establishing a daily prayer routine can bring a sense of peace, purpose, and connection to your day. To begin, choose a specific time each day that works best for you (fit Jesus into your schedule), whether it's in the morning, during a break at work, or before bed. Consistency is key in forming a habit, so try to stick to your chosen time as much as possible. Find a quiet and comfortable space where you can focus without distractions.

Getting into a routine is great however I want to be clear that it's because of Jesus' sacrifice on the cross and God giving us His only begotten Son that we are here, and we have eternal life through salvation. God, Jesus, Holy Spirit should always be the first person you want and should speak to at the beginning of you day. Before you get out your bed. Greet God, Jesus, and the Holy Spirit with a "Good Morning." This daily habit will help you cultivate a personal and intimate relationship with God, Jesus, and Holy Spirit.

Next, decide on the format of your prayers. This could include reciting traditional prayers, reading from religious texts, or simply speaking from your heart. Experiment with different styles to see what resonates most with you. Consider incorporating gratitude, reflection, requests for guidance, and intentions for the day into your prayers.

Lastly, stay open to the experience and allow your daily prayer routine to evolve naturally. It's okay to adjust your routine as needed to suit your changing needs and spiritual growth. Remember that the purpose of prayer is not just to ask for things, but also to cultivate a deeper connection with Jesus Christ.

In this section, we will explore the importance of establishing a daily prayer routine and provide practical guidance for incorporating prayer into your everyday life. By committing to a consistent prayer practice, you can deepen your relationship with God, find strength and guidance for each day, and experience the transformative power of prayer in your life.

Setting Aside Dedicated Time

Set aside dedicated time each day for prayer. Choose a time that works best for you, whether it's in the morning, during a lunch break, or before bed. Consistency is key, so aim to establish a regular prayer habit by scheduling it into your daily routine.

Creating a Sacred Space

Create a sacred space where you can pray without distractions. This could be a quiet corner in your home, a peaceful outdoor setting, or a designated prayer room.

Structuring Your Prayer Time

Structure your prayer time to include elements such as adoration, confession, thanksgiving, and supplication (ACTS). Begin by praising God for who He is, confessing any sins or shortcomings, expressing gratitude for His blessings, and presenting your requests and needs to Him in prayer.

Using Prayer Prompts or Guides

Use prayer prompts or guides to help you stay focused and intentional in your prayers. This could include prayer journals, devotional books, or smartphone apps that provide daily prompts and scriptures for prayer. Allow these resources to guide your prayers and deepen your spiritual journey.

Incorporating Different Forms of Prayer

Incorporate different forms of prayer to keep your prayer routine fresh and engaging. Experiment with techniques such as intercessory prayer, journaling, praying scripture, or prayer walks. Find what resonates with you and allows you to connect with God in a meaningful way.

Staying Flexible and Adaptable

Stay flexible and adaptable in your prayer routine, recognizing that life can be unpredictable. Be open to shifting your prayer time or location as needed to accommodate changes in your schedule or environment. The goal is not perfection but consistency and sincerity in seeking God's presence.

Persisting in Prayer

Persist in prayer even when it feels challenging or you don't see immediate results. Trust that God hears and answers your prayers according to His perfect timing and will. Lean on His promises and continue to seek His face with faith and perseverance.

Pray without ceasing. 1 Thessalonians 5:17

Prayer

Heavenly Father, thank you for the gift of prayer, through which we can commune with you and experience your presence in our lives. Guide me in establishing a daily prayer routine that draws me closer to you and deepens my relationship with you. Help me have an urgency to pray continuously. May my prayers be a fragrant offering of worship and surrender to you. In Jesus' name, amen.

4.2 Practicing Gratitude and Praise

Practicing gratitude and praise can have a profound impact on our overall well-being and outlook on life. When we take the time to acknowledge and appreciate the good things in our lives, no matter how big or small, we shift our focus from what may be lacking to what we already have. This shift in perspective can lead to increased feelings of happiness, contentment, and resilience in the face of challenges.

One way to incorporate gratitude into your daily routine is by keeping a gratitude journal. Each day, write down three things you are thankful for. This simple practice can help you cultivate a more positive mindset and become more attuned to the blessings in your life. Additionally, expressing praise and appreciation towards others not only uplifts their spirits but also strengthens your relationships and fosters a sense of connection and community.

Incorporating gratitude and praise into your life can be a powerful tool for personal growth and happiness. By making a conscious effort to focus on the positive aspects of your life and the qualities of those around you, you can cultivate a mindset of abundance and joy that will enrich your life in countless ways.

In this section, we will explore the transformative power of practicing gratitude and praise in our daily lives. By cultivating an attitude of gratitude and offering praise to God in all circumstances, we can experience joy, contentment, and a deeper connection with Him.

Cultivating a Grateful Heart

Begin by cultivating a grateful heart through intentional reflection on God's blessings. Take time each day to count your blessings, both big and small, and give thanks to God for His provision, protection, and faithfulness. Choose to focus on the good things in your life rather than dwelling on negativity or lack. The quickest way to get into the presence of God is through thanksgiving. Began to thank God for who He is. Familiarize yourself with His nature and His character, through His word.

Enter into His gates with thanksgiving, And into His courts with praise. Be thankful to Him, and bless His name. Psalms 100:4

Keeping a Gratitude Journal

Keep a gratitude journal to record daily blessings and moments of thanksgiving. Write down at least three things you are grateful for each day, along with a brief explanation of why you are thankful. Review your journal regularly to remind yourself of God's goodness and faithfulness in your life.

Offering Praise and Worship

Make praise and worship a regular part of your prayer life and personal worship. Set aside time each day to lift your voice in praise to God, expressing adoration, awe, and reverence for who He is. Sing praises, recite psalms, or simply speak words of worship from your heart. Although, I firmly believe praise is not a song. It's what you do daily through your actions. We choose to praise God or the enemy by our very words. How are you presenting yourself to God daily? Evaluate your ways, actions, mannerisms, habits, speech, and demeanour. Do they please God?

I beseech you therefore, brethren, by the mercies of God, that you present your bodies a living sacrifice, holy, acceptable to God, which is your reasonable service. Romans 12:1

Finding Beauty in the Ordinary

Find beauty in the ordinary moments of life and offer praise to God for His creation. Notice the beauty of nature, the kindness of others, and the simple pleasures that bring joy to your heart. See each moment as an opportunity to glorify God and express gratitude for His handiwork.

Practicing Gratitude in Adversity

Practice gratitude even in times of adversity and difficulty. Trust that God is working all things together for your good, even when circumstances seem bleak. Choose to thank God for His presence, His promises, and His provision, knowing that He is with you and will never leave you nor forsake you.

Sharing Your Gratitude with Others

Share your gratitude with others by expressing appreciation and encouragement. Take time to thank those who have blessed you, supported you, or shown kindness to you. Let your gratitude overflow into acts of generosity, service, and love toward others, reflecting God's love and grace.

Prayer

Heavenly Father, thank you for the countless blessings you pour out upon us each day. Help me to cultivate a grateful heart and to offer you praise and worship in all circumstances. May my life be a testament to your goodness and faithfulness, and may I always give thanks to you with a joyful heart. In Jesus' name, amen.

Seeking God's Guidance and Direction

Seeking God's guidance and direction is a common practice for many individuals seeking clarity and purpose in their lives. For those who believe in a Jesus Christ, turning to God for guidance can provide a sense of peace and assurance. One way to seek God's guidance is through prayer, where individuals can open their hearts and minds to receive divine revelation and wisdom. Reading the written word of God and seeking counsel from spiritual leaders can also offer insights and direction on important life decisions.

It is important to remember that seeking God's guidance is a personal journey that requires patience and faith. Trusting in God's plan and timing can help individuals navigate challenges and uncertainties with a sense of hope and resilience. By staying connected to one's faith and seeking guidance through prayer and reflection, individuals can find comfort and strength in knowing that they are not alone in their journey. Ultimately, seeking God's guidance can lead to a deeper sense of purpose, peace, and fulfillment in one's life.

In this section, we will explore the importance of seeking God's guidance and direction in our lives. By surrendering our plans and desires to Him and seeking His will through prayer, scripture, and discernment, we can experience His leading and walk confidently in the path He has prepared for us.

Surrendering to God's Will

Begin by surrendering your plans and desires to God, acknowledging His sovereignty and wisdom. Let go of the need to control every aspect of your life and trust that God's plans for you are good, pleasing, and perfect (Romans 12:2). Submit your will to His and invite Him to guide you in every decision and direction.

And do not be conformed to this world, but be transformed by the renewing of your mind, that you may prove what is that good and acceptable and perfect will of God. Romans 12:2

Step 2: Praying for Wisdom and Discernment

Pray for wisdom and discernment as you seek God's guidance in your life. Ask Him to grant you clarity of mind, sensitivity to His voice, and wisdom to discern His will amidst the noise and distractions of the world. Trust that He will answer your prayers and lead you in the way you should go (James 1:5).

If any of you lacks wisdom, let him ask of God, who gives to all liberally and without reproach, and it will be given to him. James 1:5

Seeking Counsel and Confirmation

Seek counsel and confirmation from trusted spiritual mentors, advisors, or friends who can offer godly wisdom and insight. Share your hopes, dreams, and concerns with them, and invite their input and prayer support as you discern God's direction. Pay attention to any patterns or themes that emerge in their advice and prayer.

Where there is no counsel, the people fall; But in the multitude of counselors there is safety. Proverbs 11:14

Listening to God's Voice

Listen attentively to God's voice as you spend time in prayer, scripture reading, and quiet reflection. Be still before Him, allowing space for His Spirit to speak to your heart and illuminate His will for your life. Tune out distractions and tune in to His voice, knowing that He delights in guiding His children (Psalm 32:8).

I will instruct you and teach you in the way you should go; I will guide you with My eye. Psalm 32:8

Aligning with God's Word

Align your desires and decisions with God's Word, using scripture as a guide for discerning His will. Search the scriptures for principles, promises, and precedents that relate to your situation, and apply them to your decision-making process. Let the truth of God's Word be a lamp to your feet and a light to your path (Psalm 119:105).

Your word is a lamp to my feet and a light to my path. Psalm 119:105

Trusting in God's Providence

Trust in God's providence and timing as you await His guidance and direction. Rest in the assurance that He is working all things together for your good, orchestrating every detail according to His perfect plan (Romans 8:28). Be patient and steadfast in prayer, knowing that He will guide you in His time and way.

And we know that all things work together for good to those who love God, to those who are the called according to His purpose. Romans 8:28

Prayer

Heavenly Father, thank you for the promise that you will guide us and direct our steps as we seek your will. Grant me wisdom and discernment to know your voice and to follow your leading in every area of my life. May I trust in your providence and surrender to your plans, knowing that you are faithful to lead me in the way I should go. In Jesus' name, amen.

4.4 Finding Strength and Comfort in His Presence

Finding strength and comfort in the presence of God or deity is a deeply personal and powerful experience for many individuals. Through through prayer, praise, and worship we can sense the glorious presence of God. It can provide a source of solace and guidance in times of need. Believers often find comfort in the idea that they are not alone in their struggles, but rather supported by a benevolent force that is always watching over them.

For some, finding strength in the presence of God can also bring a sense of purpose and meaning to their lives. It can offer a framework for understanding the world and their place in it, as well as a source of moral guidance and inspiration. Through this connection, individuals may develop a sense of gratitude, humility, and inner peace that helps them navigate life's challenges with resilience and grace.

Ultimately, the quest for strength and comfort in the presence of the God is a deeply personal journey that can take many different forms. Whether through church, or simply moments of reflection and contemplation, focusing on Jesus, you can find love and peace through His transformative and empowering when you seek Him.

In this section, we will explore the profound source of strength and comfort found in the presence of God. By drawing near to Him through prayer, worship, and meditation on His Word, you can experience His peace, assurance, and supernatural strength to face life's challenges with confidence and grace.

You will show me the path of life; In Your presence is fullness of joy; At Your right hand are pleasures forevermore. Psalms 16:11

Cultivating a Lifestyle of Presence

Begin by cultivating a lifestyle of presence, intentionally seeking God's presence in every moment of your day. Set aside dedicated time each day for prayer, worship, and scripture reading, but also strive to maintain an ongoing conversation with God throughout your daily activities.

Drawing Near to God in Prayer

Draw near to God in prayer, pouring out your heart to Him with honesty and vulnerability. Share your joys, sorrows, fears, and hopes with Him, knowing that He hears and cares for you deeply. Find solace in His presence as you cast your burdens upon Him and receive His peace that surpasses understanding (Philippians 4:6-7).

Be anxious for nothing, but in everything by prayer and supplication, with thanksgiving, let your requests be made known to God; 7 and the peace of God, which surpasses all

understanding, will guard your hearts and minds through Christ Jesus. Philippians 4:6-7

Dwelling in His Word

Dwell in God's Word as a source of strength and comfort. Meditate on scripture passages that speak to His promises, character, and faithfulness. Allow His Word to penetrate your heart and mind, renewing your strength and bolstering your faith in times of trouble (Isaiah 40:31).

But those who wait on the Lord
Shall renew their strength;
They shall mount up with wings like eagles,
They shall run and not be weary,
They shall walk and not faint.
Isaiah 40:31

Soaking in Worship and Adoration

Soak in worship and adoration as you encounter the presence of God through music, song, and praise. Lift your voice in worship, declaring His goodness, majesty, and love. Allow His Spirit to minister to your soul as you exalt His name and bask in His glory (Psalm 22:3).

But You are holy, Enthroned in the praises of Israel. Psalm 22:3

Resting in His Peace and Comfort

Rest in God's peace and comfort, knowing that He is with you in every season of life. Find refuge in His presence as you face trials, storms, and uncertainties. Allow His peace to guard your heart and mind, anchoring your soul in His unchanging love and faithfulness (John 14:27).

Peace, I leave with you, My peace I give to you; not as the world gives do I give to you. Let not your heart be troubled, neither let it be afraid. John 14:27

Drawing Strength from Community

Draw strength from the community of believers as you journey together in faith. Surround yourself with fellow sisters and brothers who can offer support, encouragement, and prayer. Share testimonies of God's faithfulness and draw inspiration from one another's experiences of finding strength and comfort in His presence.

Prayer

Heavenly Father, thank you for the gift of your presence, where we find strength, comfort, and peace beyond measure. Help me to cultivate a lifestyle of presence, drawing near to you in prayer, dwelling in your Word, and soaking in worship. May your presence be my refuge and strength in every season of life. In Jesus' name, amen.

Chapter 5: Walking in Freedom and Purpose

Walking in freedom and purpose is a journey of self-discovery and empowerment. It involves embracing your authentic self, letting go of limiting beliefs, and living in alignment with your values and passions. When you walk in freedom, you break free from the constraints of fear, doubt, and societal expectations, allowing yourself to fully express who you are and what you believe in.

Purpose gives meaning to your life and drives you towards your goals and aspirations. It is the compass that guides your decisions and actions, helping you make choices that are in line with your true calling. When you combine freedom with purpose, you create a life that is fulfilling, joyful, and deeply satisfying. It is about living intentionally, with clarity and focus, as you pursue your dreams and make a positive impact on the world around you. So, embrace your freedom, discover your purpose, and start walking confidently towards a life filled with meaning and fulfillment. YOUR ULTIMATE PURPOSE AS CHRISTIAN IS TO LOOK LIKE JESUS!

In this section, we will explore the journey of walking in freedom and purpose as women of faith. By embracing the freedom found in Christ and discovering our God-given purpose, we can live with confidence, joy, and fulfillment, making a meaningful impact in the world around us.

Embracing Freedom in Christ

Begin by embracing the freedom that is found in Christ. Recognize that through His sacrifice on the cross, you have been set free from sin, shame, and condemnation. Choose to live in the freedom that comes from knowing that you are loved, forgiven, and redeemed by Him.

Letting Go of Fear and Limiting Beliefs

Let go of fear and limiting beliefs that hold you back from walking in your full potential. Trust in God's promises and believe that He has equipped you with everything you need to fulfill His purpose for your life. Step out in faith, knowing that He is with you every step of the way.

Discovering Your God-Given Purpose

Discover your God-given purpose through prayer, reflection, and seeking God's guidance. Consider your passions, talents, and life experiences, and ask God to reveal how He wants to use them for His glory. Be open to His leading and be willing to follow wherever He may lead you.

Living with Intentionality and Purpose

Live with intentionality and purpose in every area of your life. Align your actions and decisions with God's will, seeking to honor Him in all that you do. Be proactive in pursuing opportunities to serve others, share the gospel, and make a positive impact in your sphere of influence.

Overcoming Obstacles and Opposition

Expect to face obstacles and opposition as you walk in freedom and purpose. Stand firm in your faith, knowing that God is greater than any challenge you may encounter. Lean on His strength and wisdom, and trust that He will guide you through every trial and tribulation.

Walking in Boldness and Confidence

Walk in boldness and confidence as you live out your God-given purpose. Trust in the promises of God and boldly proclaim His truth to the world around you. Let your light shine brightly, knowing that you are called to be a beacon of hope and love in a dark and broken world.

Prayer

Heavenly Father, thank you for the freedom and purpose we have in Christ. Help me to embrace this truth and walk confidently in the calling you have placed on my life. Give me the courage to let go of fear and live with boldness and intentionality, knowing that you are with me every step of the way. In Jesus' name, amen.

Letting Go of Fear and Doubt

Letting go of fear and doubt can be a transformative journey towards a more peaceful and fulfilling life. Fear and doubt are natural emotions that everyone experiences, but when they become overwhelming, they can hold us back from reaching our full potential. One way to start this process is by acknowledging and accepting these feelings without judgment. By recognizing that it's okay to feel afraid or uncertain, we can begin to release their grip on us.

Practicing mindfulness and self-compassion can also help in letting go of fear and doubt. Mindfulness involves being present in the moment and observing our thoughts and emotions without getting caught up in them. By practicing self-compassion, we learn to treat ourselves with kindness and understanding, especially when we are feeling fearful or doubtful. This can help us cultivate a sense of inner peace and resilience in the face of challenges.

Lastly, surrounding ourselves with positive and supportive influences can aid in overcoming fear and doubt. Building a strong support system of friends, family, or mentors who believe in us can provide encouragement and perspective when we are struggling. Additionally, engaging in activities that bring us joy and fulfillment can boost our confidence and self-esteem, making it easier to let go of negative emotions. Remember, letting go of fear and doubt is a process that takes time and practice, but with patience and perseverance, it is possible to create a more positive and empowering mindset.

In this section, we will explore the journey of letting go of fear and doubt and stepping into the fullness of God's promises for our lives. By surrendering our fears and doubts to Him and embracing His truth and faithfulness, we can experience freedom, peace, and confidence to live boldly for His glory.

Identifying Fear and Doubt

Begin by identifying the fears and doubts that hold you back from walking in faith and confidence. Reflect on the thoughts, beliefs, and situations that trigger feelings of fear and doubt in your life. Acknowledge them honestly before God and commit to confronting them with His help. Fear comes from the enemy, not God. Times where you feel fear is over coming you confess "God has not given me the spirit of fear, but of power love and the sound mind." The word of God is powerful!

For God has not given us a spirit of fear, but of power and of love and of a sound mind. 1 Timothy 1:7

Surrendering to God's Sovereignty

Surrender your fears and doubts to God's sovereignty and trust in His perfect plan for your life. Remember that He is in control of all things and that nothing is beyond His power or knowledge. Release your grip on control and place your trust fully in Him, knowing that He is faithful to lead you.

Renewing Your Mind with Truth

Renew your mind with the truth of God's Word to combat fear and doubt. Meditate on scriptures that speak to His faithfulness, love, and power. Replace negative thoughts and beliefs with His promises, declaring them over your life with confidence and conviction.

Stepping Out in Faith

Step out in faith, even in the face of fear and doubt. Choose to trust God's promises and obey His leading, even when it feels uncomfortable or uncertain. Remember that faith is not the absence of fear, but the courage to act in spite of it. Take small steps of obedience, trusting that God will guide you every step of the way.

For we walk by faith, not by sight. 2 Corinthians 5:7

Seeking Support and Encouragement

Seek support and encouragement from fellow believers who can walk alongside you in your journey of faith. Share your struggles and fears with trusted friends, mentors, or pastors, and invite them to pray with you and speak God's truth into your life. Allow their love and support to strengthen and uplift you.

Resting in God's Peace

Rest in God's peace as you release your fears and doubts into His hands. Trust that He is working all things together for your good, even in the midst of uncertainty and adversity. Surrender your anxieties to Him in prayer and allow His peace to guard your heart and mind (Philippians 4:6-7).

Prayer

Heavenly Father, thank you for your faithfulness and love that casts out all fear. Help me to let go of my fears and doubts and to trust fully in your sovereignty and goodness. Renew my mind with your truth and give me the courage to step out in faith, knowing that you are with me always. In Jesus' name, amen.

Stepping into God's Promises with Boldness

Stepping into God's Promises with Boldness is about embracing faith and courage as you walk on the path that God has set before you. It involves trusting in God's word and believing that He will fulfill His promises in your life. Boldness in this context means having the confidence and determination to pursue what God has in store for you, even when faced with obstacles or uncertainties.

To step into God's promises with boldness, one must first immerse themselves in prayer and seek guidance from God. By deepening your relationship with Him through regular communication and study of the Scriptures, you can better discern His will for your life.

Additionally, surrounding yourself with a supportive community of fellow believers can provide encouragement and accountability as you journey towards fulfilling God's promises.

Remember, stepping into God's promises with boldness does not necessarily mean that the path will be easy or without challenges. However, with faith, courage, and a steadfast heart, you can navigate through any trials that come your way, knowing that God's promises are true and that He is faithful to fulfill them in His perfect timing.

In this section, we will explore the journey of letting go of fear and doubt and stepping into the fullness of God's promises for our lives. By surrendering our fears and doubts to Him and embracing His truth and faithfulness, we can experience freedom, peace, and confidence to live boldly for His glory.

The wicked flee when no one pursues, But the righteous are bold as a lion. Proverbs 28:1

Identifying Fear and Doubt

Begin by identifying the fears and doubts that hold you back from walking in faith and confidence. Reflect on the thoughts, beliefs, and situations that trigger feelings of fear and doubt in your life. Acknowledge them honestly before God and commit to confronting them with His help.

Surrendering to God's Sovereignty

Surrender your fears and doubts to God's sovereignty and trust in His perfect plan for your life. Remember that He is in control of all things and that nothing is beyond His power or knowledge. Release your grip on control and place your trust fully in Him, knowing that He is faithful to lead you.

Renewing Your Mind with Truth

Renew your mind with the truth of God's Word to combat fear and doubt. Meditate on scriptures that speak to His faithfulness, love, and power. Replace negative thoughts and beliefs with His promises, declaring them over your life with confidence and conviction.

Stepping Out in Faith

Step out in faith, even in the face of fear and doubt. Choose to trust God's promises and obey His leading, even when it feels uncomfortable or uncertain. Remember that faith is not the absence of fear, but the courage to act in spite of it. Take small steps of obedience, trusting that God will guide you every step of the way.

But without faith it is impossible to please Him, for he who comes to God must believe that He is, and that He is a rewarder of those who diligently seek Him. Hebrews 11:6

Seeking Support and Encouragement

Seek support and encouragement from fellow believers who can walk alongside you in your journey of faith. Share your struggles and fears with trusted friends, mentors, or pastors, and invite them to pray with you and speak God's truth into your life. Allow their love and support to strengthen and uplift you.

Resting in God's Peace

Rest in God's peace as you release your fears and doubts into His hands. Trust that He is working all things together for your good, even in the midst of uncertainty and adversity. Surrender your anxieties to Him in prayer and allow His peace to guard your heart and mind (Philippians 4:6-7).

Prayer

Heavenly Father, thank you for your faithfulness and love that casts out all fear. Help me to let go of my fears and doubts and to trust fully in your sovereignty and goodness. I break covenant, and I renounce the authority I have given fear over my life. Renew my mind with your truth and give me the courage to step out in faith, knowing that you are with me always. In Jesus' name, amen.

Serving Others with Compassion and Grace

Serving others with compassion and grace is a noble and rewarding endeavor that can make a significant difference in people's lives. Compassion involves showing empathy and understanding towards others, acknowledging their struggles and offering support without judgment. It's about putting yourself in someone else's shoes and responding with kindness and care.

Grace, on the other hand, involves approaching situations with poise, dignity, and respect. It means treating others with courtesy and consideration, even in challenging circumstances. Combining compassion and grace in your interactions can create a powerful impact, uplifting those around you and fostering a sense of connection and community.

Whether it's through volunteering, lending a listening ear, or simply offering a helping hand, serving others with compassion and grace can not only brighten someone else's day but also enrich your own life in ways you may not even expect. It's a reminder of our shared humanity and the beauty of kindness in a world that can sometimes feel chaotic and overwhelming.

In this section, we will explore the transformative power of serving others with compassion and grace. By following the example of Jesus Christ and extending love and kindness to those in need, women can make a meaningful impact in their communities and reflect the heart of God to the world.

Embracing the Call to Serve

Begin by embracing the call to serve others as a reflection of God's love and compassion. Recognize that serving is not just a duty, but a privilege and an opportunity to demonstrate Christ-like humility and selflessness. Open your heart to the needs of those around you and be willing to respond with love and compassion.

Cultivating a Heart of Compassion

Cultivate a heart of compassion by seeing others through the eyes of Christ. Take time to listen to their stories, empathize with their struggles, and extend kindness and empathy. Let your heart be moved with compassion for the broken, the marginalized, and the hurting, just as Jesus' heart was moved (Matthew 9:36).

Practicing Acts of Kindness

Practice acts of kindness in your daily life, both big and small. Look for opportunities to bless others with words of encouragement, acts of service, or gestures of generosity. Whether it's lending a listening ear, offering a helping hand, or providing practical support, let your actions reflect the love of Christ.

Extending Forgiveness and Grace

Extend forgiveness and grace to those who have wronged you, just as Christ has forgiven you. Release bitterness, resentment, and judgment, and choose to forgive others as Christ has forgiven you (Ephesians 4:32). Let go of the need for revenge or retribution, and instead offer grace and reconciliation.

Serving with Humility and Joy

Serve others with humility and joy, knowing that you are following in the footsteps of your Savior. Approach each opportunity to serve with a humble attitude, considering others as more important than yourself (Philippians 2:3). Find joy in the privilege of serving, knowing that you are storing up treasures in heaven (Matthew 6:20).

Making a Lasting Impact

Make a lasting impact in your community and beyond through your acts of service and compassion. Partner with local organizations, ministries, or churches to serve those in need, and look for ways to address systemic issues of injustice and inequality. Be a voice for the voiceless and an advocate for the vulnerable, shining the light of Christ in a dark world.

Prayer

Heavenly Father, thank you for the privilege of serving others with compassion and grace. Help me to cultivate a heart of compassion, extend forgiveness and grace, and serve with humility and joy. Use me to make a lasting impact in my community and to bring glory to your name. In Jesus' name, amen.

Embracing Your Calling and Mission in Christ

Embracing your calling and mission in Christ is a deeply personal and spiritual journey that involves understanding and following the path that God has laid out for you. It requires introspection, prayer, and discernment to discover what unique gifts and talents you have been blessed with and how you can use them to serve others and glorify God. By aligning your will with God's will, you can find fulfillment and purpose in carrying out the mission that has been entrusted to you.

One key aspect of embracing your calling and mission in Christ is to cultivate a deep relationship with God through prayer, study of scripture, and participation in the sacraments. By staying connected to God and seeking His guidance, you can gain the strength and wisdom needed to fulfill your mission with courage and conviction. Additionally, being open to the Holy Spirit's promptings and being willing to step out of your comfort zone to answer God's call is essential in living out your purpose in Christ.

Remember that embracing your calling and mission in Christ is not always easy, and there may be challenges and obstacles along the way. However, by trusting in God's plan for your life, staying rooted in faith, and relying on the support of fellow believers, you can navigate through difficulties and continue to walk in the path that God has set before you. Ultimately, by embracing your calling and mission in Christ, you can experience a profound sense of joy, peace, and fulfillment as you live out God's purpose for your life.

In this section, we will explore the journey of embracing your calling and mission in Christ. By discovering and embracing the unique purpose and mission that God has for your life, you can experience fulfillment, joy, and impact as you live out your faith in obedience to His will.

And the Lord called Samuel again the third time. So, he arose and went to Eli, and said, "Here I am, for you did call me." Then Eli perceived that the Lord had called the boy. 1 Samuel 3:8

Seeking God's Guidance

Begin by seeking God's guidance in discerning your calling and mission. Spend time in prayer, asking God to reveal His purpose for your life and to guide you in the steps you should take. Be open to His leading and trust that He will make His plans known to you in His perfect timing.

Discovering Your Gifts and Passions

Discover your gifts, talents, and passions as clues to your calling and mission. Reflect on the activities and pursuits that bring you the greatest joy and fulfillment, as well as the areas where you excel. Consider how you can use your unique abilities to glorify God and serve others in the context of your calling.

Aligning with God's Word

Align your calling and mission with God's Word and His purposes for His kingdom. Ensure that your aspirations and goals are in line with the principles and values of the Bible, and seek to honor God in all that you do. Let His Word be a lamp to your feet and a light to your path as you navigate your calling.

Stepping Out in Faith

Step out in faith as you pursue your calling and mission in Christ. Trust in God's provision and guidance, even when the path ahead seems uncertain or challenging. Take bold steps of obedience, knowing that God is faithful to equip and empower you for the work He has prepared for you (Ephesians 2:10).

For we are His workmanship, created in Christ Jesus for good works, which God prepared beforehand that we should walk in them. Ephesians 2:10

Embracing Your Identity in Christ

Embrace your identity in Christ as the foundation of your calling and mission. Remember that you are a beloved child of God, chosen and appointed to bear fruit that will last (John 15:16). Find your worth and significance in Him, rather than in external achievements or recognition.

You did not choose Me, but I chose you and appointed you that you should go and bear fruit, and that your fruit should remain, that whatever you ask the Father in My name He may give you. John 15:16

Making an Impact for His Kingdom

Make an impact for His kingdom as you live out your calling and mission with passion and purpose. Use your gifts and talents to serve others, share the gospel, and advance God's purposes in the world. Be faithful in the little things, trusting that God will use your obedience to bring about His kingdom purposes.

Prayer

Heavenly Father, thank you for calling me and equipping me for a purpose that is unique and significant. Guide me in discovering and embracing my calling and mission in Christ, and empower me to live out my faith with passion and purpose. May all that I do bring glory to your name and advance your kingdom. In Jesus' name, amen.

Chapter 6: Building Healthy Relationships

Building healthy relationships that are Christ-centered is a fundamental aspect of many people's lives. In these types of relationships, individuals look to Jesus Christ as a model for how to treat others with love, respect, and compassion. By following Christ's teachings, individuals can cultivate relationships that are grounded in faith, trust, and mutual understanding.

In a Christ-centered relationship, communication plays a vital role. Open and honest communication allows individuals to express their thoughts, feelings, and concerns in a respectful manner. By listening actively and empathetically to one another, partners can deepen their connection and strengthen their bond. Additionally, practicing forgiveness and grace, as Christ exemplified, can help couples navigate challenges and conflicts with humility and understanding.

Furthermore, prayer and spiritual growth are essential components of a Christ-centered relationship. By praying together, seeking God's guidance, and growing in faith side by side, couples can support each other in their spiritual journeys and strengthen their relationship with each other and with God. Ultimately, building a healthy, Christ-centered relationship requires commitment, patience, and a shared dedication to living out the principles of love and grace that Christ taught.

Building healthy relationships is essential for our well-being and happiness. Communication is a key component in any healthy relationship. It's important to express your thoughts and feelings openly and honestly, while also listening to your partner with empathy and understanding. This creates a safe space for both individuals to share their concerns and work through any challenges together.

Another crucial aspect of a healthy relationship is mutual respect. Both parties should respect each other's boundaries, opinions, and differences. It's important to treat each other with kindness, appreciation, and support. Trust is also fundamental in building a strong and healthy relationship. Trusting your friend or partner and being trustworthy yourself fosters a sense of security and intimacy in the relationship.

Additionally, spending quality time together, showing affection, and appreciating each other's efforts can strengthen the bond between partners. It's important to nurture the relationship by being attentive, understanding, and willing to compromise when necessary. By prioritizing open communication, respect, trust, and love, you can build a healthy and fulfilling relationship that stands the test of time.

The greatest act of kindness is love. We are called to love our neighbor as ourselves. Through healing and wholeness in Christ you will find the true love of Father and that is the same love God wants you to extend to others. When I love my brother, sister, friend, spouse, and family as I love myself I extend grace and love to them. I'm careful and caution of how I talk to them. Yes, you will still make mistake however a person filled with the love of Jesus will always be quick to ask for forgive and repent. God knows you will still make mistakes this why we need Jesus. He is the perfect example of love.

In this section, we will explore the importance of building healthy relationships and nurturing meaningful connections with others. By cultivating empathy, communication skills, and mutual respect, women can create strong, supportive relationships that enrich their lives and bring glory to God.

You shall love your neighbor as yourself. Matthew 22:39

Cultivating Empathy and Compassion

Begin by cultivating empathy and compassion towards others. Seek to understand their perspectives, feelings, and experiences, and respond with kindness and empathy. Practice active listening and validate their emotions, showing them that they are seen, heard, and valued.

Communicating Effectively

Communicate effectively in your relationships by expressing yourself openly and honestly, while also listening attentively to others. Practice clear and respectful communication, and strive to resolve conflicts peacefully and constructively. Be willing to compromise and seek understanding, rather than insisting on being right.

Setting Healthy Boundaries

Set healthy boundaries in your relationships to protect your emotional well-being and maintain healthy dynamics. Clearly communicate your needs, preferences, and limits to others, and assertively enforce boundaries when necessary. Respect the boundaries of others and strive to create a safe and respectful environment for all parties involved.

Investing Time and Effort

Invest time and effort into nurturing your relationships and building strong connections with others. Prioritize quality time spent together, whether it's through meaningful conversations, shared activities, or acts of service. Show appreciation for the people in your life and make an effort to stay connected, even during busy seasons.

Practicing Forgiveness and Grace

Practice forgiveness and grace in your relationships, recognizing that everyone makes mistakes and falls short at times. Choose to extend grace to others, just as you have received grace from God. Let go of resentment and bitterness, and instead offer forgiveness and reconciliation, as Christ has forgiven you.

Then he said, "If now I have found grace in Your sight, O Lord, let my Lord, I pray, go among us, even though we are a stiff-necked people; and pardon our iniquity and our

sin, and take us as Your inheritance." Exodus 34:9

Seeking God's Guidance

Seek God's guidance in your relationships, inviting His wisdom and grace to guide your interactions and decisions. Pray for wisdom, discernment, and patience as you navigate the complexities of relationships. Trust that God is at work in your relationships, bringing healing, growth, and reconciliation where needed.

Building a Community of Support

Build a community of support around you by nurturing relationships with family, friends, mentors, and fellow believers. Surround yourself with people who uplift and encourage you, and who share your values and faith. Lean on your community for support during difficult times, and be a source of strength and encouragement to others in return.

Prayer

Heavenly Father, thank you for the gift of relationships, through which we experience love, support, and connection. Help me to build healthy relationships based on empathy, communication, and mutual respect. Guide me in setting healthy boundaries, practicing forgiveness, and seeking your wisdom in all my interactions. May my relationships be a reflection of your love and grace to the world. In Jesus' name, amen.

Setting Boundaries with Love and Wisdom

Setting boundaries with love and wisdom is an essential skill in maintaining healthy relationships and protecting your well-being. Boundaries are the guidelines we set for ourselves in how we allow others to treat us, how we interact with others, and how we take care of ourselves. It is important to establish boundaries with kindness and respect for yourself and others.

When setting boundaries, it is crucial to communicate them clearly and assertively. Express your needs, feelings, and limits in a calm and respectful manner. Be open to listening to the other person's perspective and try to find a compromise that respects both parties. Remember that setting boundaries is not about controlling others but about taking care of yourself and fostering healthy relationships.

Setting boundaries with love and wisdom involves self-awareness, self-respect, and empathy. It requires understanding your own needs and priorities, respecting yourself enough to enforce those boundaries, and empathizing with others while maintaining your own well-being. By setting boundaries with love and wisdom, you can cultivate healthier relationships, reduce stress, and create a more peaceful and fulfilling life for yourself and those around you.

In this section, we will explore the importance of setting boundaries with love and wisdom in our relationships. By establishing healthy boundaries grounded in God's love and guided by His wisdom, women can protect their well-being, nurture healthy connections, and honor God in their interactions with others.

Understanding the Purpose of Boundaries

Begin by understanding the purpose of boundaries in relationships. Recognize that boundaries are not barriers to keep people out, but rather guidelines to define healthy interaction and protect personal well-being. Understand that setting boundaries is an act of self-care and a means of fostering healthier, more respectful relationships.

Identifying Your Needs and Limits

Identify your needs, preferences, and limits in various areas of your life and relationships. Reflect on what makes you feel comfortable, respected, and valued, as well as situations or behaviors that cause you discomfort or distress. Use this self-awareness to establish clear boundaries that honor your well-being and values.

Communicating Boundaries Effectively

Communicate your boundaries effectively and assertively with others. Clearly articulate your needs, preferences, and limits in a respectful and non-confrontational manner. Use "I" statements to express how certain behaviors or situations impact you personally, and be open to discussing and negotiating boundaries collaboratively.

Enforcing Boundaries Consistently

Enforce your boundaries consistently and assertively when they are crossed. Respectfully but firmly assert your boundaries and communicate consequences for violating them. Be prepared to follow through with consequences if necessary, in order to uphold the integrity of your boundaries and protect your well-being.

Extending Grace and Understanding

Extend grace and understanding to others when they struggle to respect your boundaries. Recognize that boundary-setting is a process, and that others may need time to adjust to your boundaries and understand their importance. Offer patience, empathy, and guidance as you navigate boundaries together.

Seeking God's Wisdom and Guidance

Seek God's wisdom and guidance as you establish and enforce boundaries in your relationships. Pray for discernment and clarity in recognizing healthy boundaries, and for strength and courage to uphold them with love and wisdom. Trust in God's provision and protection as you prioritize your well-being and honor Him in your interactions with others.

Reflecting God's Love and Grace

Reflect God's love and grace in your boundary-setting by demonstrating kindness, compassion, and understanding towards others. Approach boundary-setting from a place of love and concern for both yourself and the other person, seeking mutual respect and understanding in your relationships. Let your boundaries be a reflection of God's love and wisdom at work in your life.

Prayer

Heavenly Father, thank you for the wisdom and guidance you offer us as we navigate relationships and set boundaries. Help me to establish boundaries with love and wisdom, honoring both myself and others in the process. Grant me strength and grace to enforce boundaries consistently and assertively, and may my relationships reflect your love and grace to the world. In Jesus' name, amen.

Extending Forgiveness and Grace to Others

Extending forgiveness and grace to others is a noble and powerful act that can bring healing and peace to both the giver and the recipient. Forgiveness involves letting go of feelings of anger, resentment, or revenge towards someone who has wronged you. It does not mean condoning or excusing the behavior, but rather choosing to release the negative emotions associated with the hurt. By forgiving others, you free yourself from the burden of carrying around negative emotions and allow yourself to move forward with a sense of peace and closure.

Grace, on the other hand, involves showing kindness, compassion, and understanding towards others, even when they may not deserve it. It means offering love and empathy instead of judgment and condemnation. By extending grace to others, you create a space for healing, growth, and reconciliation. It can foster a sense of connection and understanding between people, leading to stronger relationships and a more harmonious environment. In a world where conflicts and misunderstandings are common, choosing to extend forgiveness and grace can be a powerful way to promote peace and understanding.

In this section, we will explore the transformative power of extending forgiveness and grace to others in our relationships. By following the example of Christ and embracing forgiveness as a cornerstone of our interactions, women can experience healing, reconciliation, and deeper connections with those around them.

Understanding the Gift of Forgiveness

Begin by understanding the profound gift of forgiveness that God has extended to us through Christ. Reflect on the depth of God's grace and mercy towards us, despite our shortcomings and failures. Recognize that forgiveness is not condoning or excusing wrongdoing, but releasing the hold of bitterness and resentment in order to experience freedom and healing.

Reflecting on Your Own Need for Grace

Reflect on your own need for grace and forgiveness in your life. Acknowledge times when you have fallen short or caused harm to others, and consider the forgiveness and grace that you have received from God and from others. Let this awareness humble you and fuel your desire to extend the same grace to others.

Choosing to Forgive

Choose to forgive others, even when it is difficult or painful. Make a conscious decision to release feelings of anger, resentment, and bitterness towards those who have hurt you, entrusting justice and reconciliation to God. Remember that forgiveness is a process, and it may require time and effort to fully let go of hurt and pain. Forgive by faith. Release those individuals into the blessing and favor of the Lord. Forgive, for you to have been forgive. People have the propensity to forget what they did to you. While you harbor unforgiveness in your heart, majority of people have moved on with their lives. People quickly forget. Don't allow unforgiveness to linger any longer. Uproot unforgiveness and take back your power and destiny.

Letting Go of Resentment and Bitterness

Let go of resentment and bitterness as you forgive others. Release the desire for revenge or retaliation, and instead choose to bless and pray for those who have wronged you (Matthew 5:44). Allow God's grace to heal the wounds of the past and replace them with His peace and restoration. Be quick to forgive as you go forward in life. Offense will always lead to unforgiveness.

Extending Grace and Compassion

Extend grace and compassion to others, just as Christ has extended it to you. Show kindness, understanding, and empathy towards those who have hurt you, recognizing that they, too, are in need of God's grace and forgiveness. Seek to build bridges of reconciliation and restoration in your relationships. Just as Christ had to forgive as He hung on the cross. The same people to put Him to death. He had to forgive. His assignment wouldn't have been ineffective and incomplete. Destiny assignments cannot be fulfilled where there is unforgiveness. What assignments have you indirectly mishandled or forfeited through unforgiveness?

Setting Healthy Boundaries

Set healthy boundaries in your relationships as you extend forgiveness and grace to others. While forgiveness is essential for reconciliation, it does not always mean restoring the relationship to its previous state. Evaluate the dynamics of the relationship and establish boundaries that protect your emotional well-being and foster healthy interactions.

Trusting in God's Sovereignty

Trust in God's sovereignty and faithfulness as you navigate the complexities of forgiveness and grace. Surrender your hurts and struggles to Him, knowing that He is able to redeem and restore even the most broken relationships. Lean on His strength and guidance as you extend forgiveness and grace to others, trusting that He will work all things together for good (Romans 8:28).

Prayer

Heavenly Father, thank you for the gift of forgiveness and grace that we have received through Christ. Help me to extend that same forgiveness and grace to others in my life.

Give me the strength to let go of resentment and bitterness, and the courage to build bridges of reconciliation and restoration in my relationships. May your love and grace shine through me in all that I do. In Jesus' name, amen.

Cultivating Authentic Connections with Sisters in Christ

Cultivating authentic connections with sisters in Christ is a beautiful and meaningful endeavor that can bring immense joy and support to your life. To build genuine relationships with your fellow sisters in Christ, it's important to prioritize honesty, vulnerability, and empathy. Share your struggles, triumphs, and dreams with each other, creating a safe space for open communication and understanding.

One way to foster these connections is through regular prayer and Bible study together. By delving into God's word as a group, you can deepen your spiritual bond and gain insights and wisdom that can strengthen your relationships. Additionally, serving together in your community or church can provide opportunities for teamwork, fellowship, and shared experiences that will further solidify your connections.

Lastly, remember to practice active listening and provide encouragement and support to your sisters in Christ. Celebrate each other's successes, offer a listening ear during challenging times, and uplift one another through prayer and acts of kindness. By investing time and effort into cultivating these authentic connections, you can create a sisterhood that reflects the love and grace of Christ.

In this section, we will explore the importance of cultivating authentic connections with sisters in Christ. By fostering genuine relationships grounded in love, support, and mutual faith, women can experience deep spiritual growth, encouragement, and community as they journey together in their faith.

Recognizing the Value of Sisterhood

Begin by recognizing the immense value of sisterhood in the body of Christ. Understand that God designed us for community and fellowship, and that authentic connections with other believers can strengthen our faith and provide invaluable support and encouragement along our spiritual journey.

Creating a Safe and Welcoming Environment

Create a safe and welcoming environment where sisters in Christ feel accepted, valued, and loved. Foster an atmosphere of authenticity, vulnerability, and non-judgmental acceptance, where women can share their joys, struggles, and doubts without fear of rejection or condemnation.

Investing Time and Effort

Invest time and effort into building and nurturing relationships with sisters in Christ. Prioritize quality time spent together, whether it's through regular gatherings, shared activities, or one-on-one conversations. Be intentional about reaching out and connecting with others, even in the midst of busy schedules.

Practicing Active Listening and Empathy

Practice active listening and empathy in your interactions with sisters in Christ. Seek to understand their perspectives, feelings, and experiences, and respond with compassion, kindness, and understanding. Show genuine interest in their lives and struggles, and offer support and encouragement as needed.

Sharing Your Journey and Faith

Share your own journey and faith with sisters in Christ, being open and transparent about your struggles, victories, and questions. Create opportunities for authentic sharing and spiritual growth, such as through Bible studies, prayer groups, or discipleship relationships. Let your vulnerability and authenticity inspire others to do the same.

Supporting and Encouraging One Another

Support and encourage one another in your walk with Christ. Be a source of strength and encouragement to sisters in Christ, praying for them, speaking truth and life into their situations, and walking alongside them through both joys and sorrows. Build each other up in faith and love, spurring one another on toward love and good deeds (Hebrews 10:24).

Praying Together and for Each Other

Pray together and for each other, lifting up your needs, concerns, and praises to God in prayer. Make prayer a central part of your relationships, seeking God's guidance, wisdom, and provision for each other's lives. Experience the power of united prayer as you support and intercede for one another in love.

Prayer

Heavenly Father, thank you for the gift of sisterhood in Christ, through which we experience love, support, and encouragement on our spiritual journey. Help me to cultivate authentic connections with sisters in Christ, fostering a community of faith, love, and mutual support. May our relationships bring glory to your name and build up your kingdom. In Jesus' name, amen.

Nurturing Family and Community with God's Love

Nurturing family and community with God's love is a beautiful and powerful concept that emphasizes the importance of love, compassion, and unity in our relationships with our loved ones and neighbors. When we center our interactions with others around God's love, we are reminded to show kindness, forgiveness, and understanding in all our interactions. This love serves as a foundation for building strong, supportive families and close-knit communities where everyone feels valued and cared for.

In a family setting, God's love can be exemplified through patience, respect, and selflessness towards one another. By practicing these values, family members can create a harmonious and loving environment where each individual feels heard, understood, and accepted. This nurturing atmosphere not only strengthens family bonds but also instills important values in children, teaching them the significance of love and empathy in their relationships with others.

Similarly, in our communities, God's love can inspire acts of service, generosity, and inclusivity towards those around us. By reaching out to our neighbors with kindness and compassion, we can create a sense of belonging and support that enriches the lives of all community members. Through nurturing family and community with God's love, we can cultivate a culture of care and unity that uplifts and sustains us in times of joy and challenges alike.

In this section, we will explore the transformative power of nurturing family and community with God's love. By fostering environments of love, support, and unity within our families and communities, women can create spaces where individuals thrive, relationships flourish, and God's kingdom is advanced.

For as we have many members in one body, but all the members do not have the same function. Romans 12:4

Embracing God's Love

Begin by embracing God's love as the foundation for nurturing family and community. Understand that God's love is unconditional, sacrificial, and transformative, and allow it to flow through you to those around you. Let His love be the guiding force in your interactions and relationships.

Prioritizing Relationships

Prioritize relationships within your family and community, investing time and effort into nurturing meaningful connections with loved ones and neighbors. Make intentional choices to spend quality time together, engage in meaningful conversations, and support one another in both joys and challenges.

Creating a Culture of Grace

Create a culture of grace within your family and community, where forgiveness, acceptance, and compassion abound. Recognize that everyone falls short at times and extend grace to one another as Christ has extended it to you. Foster an environment where mistakes are opportunities for growth and reconciliation.

Practicing Servant Leadership

Practice servant leadership within your family and community, following the example of Jesus Christ who came not to be served, but to serve (Mark 10:45). Seek opportunities to serve and uplift others, putting their needs and well-being above your own. Lead with humility, compassion, and integrity.

For even the Son of Man did not come to be served, but to serve, and to give His life a ransom for many. Mark 10:45

Cultivating Unity and Harmony

Cultivate unity and harmony within your family and community, celebrating diversity and embracing each person's unique gifts and contributions. Foster open communication, collaboration, and mutual respect, striving to build bridges of understanding and reconciliation where there is division or discord.

So, we being many, are one body in Christ, and individually members of one another. Romans 12:5

Extending Hospitality and Generosity

Extend hospitality and generosity to those within your family and community, welcoming others into your home and your life with open arms. Share your time, resources, and talents generously, seeking to meet the practical and emotional needs of those around you. Create a culture of generosity and abundance that reflects God's heart for hospitality.

Give, and it will be given to you: good measure, pressed down, shaken together, and running over will be put into your bosom. For with the same measure that you use, it will be measured back to you. Luke 6:38

Praying for Each Other

Pray for each other within your family and community, lifting up their needs, concerns, and praises to God in prayer. Make prayer a central part of your relationships, seeking God's guidance, wisdom, and provision for each other's lives. Experience the power of united prayer as you support and intercede for one another in love. God requires us to pray for our enemies, that means those that have hurt us, cause pain, trauma, lied, manipulated, and deceived us. We are to pray for them. I have learned through life and experience that true forgiveness is praying for your enemies. If you aren't able to pray for some that means you truly haven't forgiven that individual.

Prayer

Heavenly Father, thank you for the gift of family and community, through which we experience the richness of life and the depth of your love. Help me to nurture relationships with love, grace, and humility, fostering environments where individuals thrive and your kingdom is advanced. May our families and communities be beacons of your love and grace to the world. In Jesus' name, amen.

Chapter 7: Trusting God's Timing and Plan

Trusting in God's timing and plan can be a source of comfort and strength during challenging times. It requires having faith that everything happens for a reason and that there is a greater purpose behind the events unfolding in our lives. By surrendering control and letting go of our own expectations, we can find peace in the belief that God's plan is ultimately for our good.

It's important to remember that God's timing may not align with our own desires or timelines. Patience and trust are key components of this process, as we wait for things to unfold in the way they are meant to. Through prayer, reflection, and seeking guidance from spiritual mentors, we can deepen our connection to God and better understand His plan for us. Ultimately, trusting in God's timing and plan can lead to a sense of peace, purpose, and fulfillment in our lives.

In this section, we will explore the profound journey of trusting God's timing and plan in our lives. By surrendering our desires, fears, and uncertainties to Him, women can experience peace, fulfillment, and purpose as they walk in faith and obedience to His will.

Surrendering Control

Begin by surrendering control of your life and circumstances to God. Recognize that His ways are higher than our ways, and His thoughts are higher than our thoughts (Isaiah 55:8-9). Let go of the need to understand or manipulate every aspect of your life, and trust in His sovereignty and goodness.

For My thoughts are not your thoughts, nor are your ways My ways, says the Lord. For as the heavens are higher than the earth, so are

My ways higher than your ways, and My thoughts than your thoughts. Isaiah 55:8-9

Embracing God's Timing

Embrace God's timing in your life, even when it differs from your own expectations or desires. Understand that God operates according to His perfect timing, which may not always align with our plans or schedules. Trust that He knows what is best for you and that His timing is always perfect.

To everything there is a season, a time for every purpose under heaven: A time to be born, and a time to die; A time to plant, and a time to pluck what is planted; A time to kill, and a time to heal; A time to break down, and a time to build up; A time to weep, and a time to laugh; A time to mourn, and a time to dance; A time to cast away stones, and a time to gather stones; A time to embrace, and a time to refrain from embracing; A time to gain, and a time to lose; A time to keep, and a time to throw away; A time to tear, and a time to sew; A time to keep silence, and a time to speak; A

time to love, and a time to hate; A time of war, and a time of peace. Ecclesiastes 3:1-8

Step 3: Seeking God's Will

Seek God's will and guidance in every area of your life, through prayer, meditation on His Word, and seeking counsel from wise and godly mentors. Align your desires and aspirations with His purposes and priorities, trusting that He will direct your steps and lead you in the way you should go (Proverbs 3:5-6).

Trust in the Lord with all your heart, and lean not on your own understanding; In all your ways acknowledge Him, and He shall direct your paths. Proverbs 3:5-6

Finding Peace in Uncertainty

Find peace in the midst of uncertainty by resting in God's promises and character. Remember that He is faithful and trustworthy, and that He has promised to never leave us nor forsake us (Hebrews 13:5). Cast your anxieties on Him, knowing that He cares for you (1 Peter 5:7), and allow His peace to guard your heart and mind in Christ Jesus (Philippians 4:7).

Let your conduct be without covetousness; be content with such things as you have. For He Himself has said, I will never leave you nor forsake you. Hebrews 13:5

Letting Go of Comparison

Let go of comparison and the pressure to measure up to others' timelines or accomplishments. Trust that God has a unique plan and purpose for your life, tailored specifically to who you are and the gifts

He has given you. Focus on being faithful and obedient to His calling, rather than striving to meet worldly standards of success or achievement.

Waiting with Expectation

Wait with expectation and anticipation for God to fulfill His promises in your life. Be vigilant in prayer and attentive to His leading, trusting that He is working behind the scenes to bring about His purposes. Cultivate a spirit of hope and expectancy, knowing that God is able to do immeasurably more than all we ask or imagine (Ephesians 3:20).

Now to Him who is able to do exceedingly abundantly above all that we ask or think, according to the power that works in us.
Ephesians 3:20

Praising God in Every Season

Praise God in every season of life, whether in times of abundance or times of scarcity, in times of joy or times of sorrow. Rejoice in His goodness, faithfulness, and sovereignty, knowing that He is working all things together for your good and His glory (Romans 8:28). Let your praise be a testament to your trust in His timing and plan.

Prayer

Heavenly Father, thank you for your perfect timing and plan for my life. Help me to trust in your sovereignty and goodness, even when life feels uncertain or out of control. Give me the faith to surrender my desires and fears to you, and the patience to wait for your timing. May your will be done in my life, for your glory and my good. In Jesus' name, amen.

Surrendering Your Desires and Plans to God

Surrendering your desires and plans to God can be a profound act of faith and trust. It involves letting go of your own will and entrusting your life to God. This surrender can bring a sense of peace and freedom, knowing that you are not alone in navigating life's challenges. It requires humility to acknowledge that God's plans may be different from your own, but believing that His ways are ultimately for your good.

Practicing surrender can involve prayer and reflection on scripture. It's about aligning your heart with God's will and being open to His guidance. Surrendering doesn't mean giving up on your dreams, but rather being receptive to the path that God has in store for you. It's a journey of faith that can lead to a deeper relationship with the divine and a sense of purpose in following His direction.

In this section, we will explore the profound journey of surrendering your desires and plans to God. By relinquishing control and submitting to His will, women can experience freedom, peace, and fulfillment as they align their lives with His purposes and priorities.

Recognizing God's Sovereignty

Begin by recognizing God's sovereignty over your life and circumstances. Understand that He is the Creator and Sustainer of all things, and that His plans and purposes far surpass our own (Isaiah 55:8-9). Acknowledge His authority and wisdom, and trust that His ways are always higher and better than ours.

Letting Go of Control

Let go of the need to control every aspect of your life and future. Surrender your desires, plans, and ambitions to God, trusting that He knows what is best for you. Release the burden of trying to orchestrate outcomes according to your own understanding, and instead entrust yourself fully into His loving care.

Yielding to His Will

Yield to God's will in every area of your life, seeking His guidance and direction in your decisions and actions. Submit your plans and aspirations to Him, inviting His Spirit to lead and guide you along the path He has prepared for you. Be willing to follow wherever He leads, even if it means stepping into the unknown or letting go of cherished dreams.

Embracing His Purposes

Embrace God's purposes for your life, recognizing that they are always good, pleasing, and perfect (Romans 12:2). Trust that He has a unique and meaningful plan for you, one that is designed to bring glory to His name and blessing to your life. Align your desires and ambitions with His purposes, and find fulfillment in walking in obedience to Him.

Finding Peace in Surrender

Find peace in the act of surrendering your desires and plans to God. Rest in the assurance that He is faithful and trustworthy, and that He will never lead you astray. Experience the freedom that comes from releasing the burden of trying to control outcomes, and instead entrusting yourself into His loving and capable hands.

Come to me, all you who are weary and burdened, and I will give you rest. 29 Take my yoke upon you and learn from me, for I am gentle and humble in heart, and you will find rest for your souls. 30 For my yoke is easy and my burden is light. Matthew 11:28-30

Seeking His Presence

Seek God's presence and guidance daily through prayer, meditation on His Word, and fellowship with other believers. Cultivate a heart that is sensitive to His leading, and be attentive to the promptings of

His Spirit within you. Trust that He will direct your steps and order your path as you seek Him with all your heart (Proverbs 3:5-6).

Resting in His Love

Rest in the love and grace of God, knowing that He cares for you deeply and desires the best for your life. Let go of anxiety, fear, and doubt, and instead trust in His unfailing love and provision. Allow His peace to guard your heart and mind, and find contentment in knowing that you are held securely in His embrace.

Prayer

Heavenly Father, thank you for the privilege of surrendering my desires and plans to you. Help me to release control and trust in your sovereign will and purposes for my life. Give me the strength and courage to yield to your leading, and the peace that surpasses all understanding as I rest in your love and care. May your will be done in my life, for your glory and my good. In Jesus' name, amen.

Resting in His Perfect Peace and Provision

Resting in the perfect peace and provision of God or divine being can bring a sense of calm and security to individuals facing challenges or uncertainties in life. This state of rest is often associated with letting go of worries and trusting in a greater plan or purpose. By surrendering control and allowing oneself to be taken care of, individuals can experience a profound sense of peace that transcends understanding.

Finding rest in the midst of chaos can be a powerful practice for mental, emotional, and spiritual well-being. It involves cultivating a mindset of gratitude, acceptance, and mindfulness, focusing on the present moment rather than dwelling on past regrets or future anxieties. Through prayer, meditation on the word, or simply quiet reflection, individuals can connect with a sense of inner peace that provides strength and resilience in the face of adversity. Ultimately, resting in perfect peace and provision is a choice to trust in something beyond oneself and to embrace the journey with faith and hope.

In this section, we will explore the profound peace and provision that comes from resting in God's perfect care. By entrusting our lives completely to Him and relying on His faithfulness, women can experience a deep sense of security, contentment, and joy regardless of their circumstances.

Surrendering to God's Sovereignty

Begin by surrendering to God's sovereignty over your life and circumstances. Acknowledge His infinite wisdom and power, recognizing that He is in control of all things and that His plans for you are good and purposeful (Jeremiah 29:11). Release your worries and fears into His capable hands, trusting in His loving care.

Letting Go of Anxiety

Let go of anxiety and worry, casting all your cares upon the Lord, for He cares for you (1 Peter 5:7). Recognize that anxiety stems from a lack of trust in God's provision and a desire to control outcomes. Choose instead to place your trust in Him, knowing that He is faithful to meet all your needs according to His riches in glory (Philippians 4:19).

Trusting in His Provision

Trust in God's provision for your every need, both spiritual and material. Have faith that He knows what you need before you even ask Him (Matthew 6:8), and that He is able to supply all your needs according to His riches in Christ Jesus (Philippians 4:19). Rely on His faithfulness to provide for you in ways that are far beyond what you could ask or imagine.

Therefore, do not be like them. For your Father knows the things you have need of before you ask Him. Matthew 6:8

Step 4: Seeking His Kingdom First

Seek God's kingdom and righteousness above all else, trusting that He will take care of everything else (Matthew 6:33). Make it your highest priority to honor God with your life and to pursue His purposes and priorities. Trust that as you seek Him first, He will guide your steps and provide for all your needs in His perfect timing and way.

But seek first the kingdom of God and His righteousness, and all these things shall be added to you. Matthew 6:33

Resting in His Promises

Rest in the promises of God, knowing that they are true and unchanging. Meditate on His Word day and night, allowing His promises to fill your heart with faith and confidence. Claim His promises of peace, provision, and protection over your life, and trust that He is faithful to fulfill every word He has spoken.

Abiding in His Presence

Abide in God's presence through prayer, worship, and fellowship with Him. Cultivate a deep and intimate relationship with Him, spending time in His presence daily and allowing His Spirit to fill you with His peace and joy. Find rest for your soul in His presence, knowing that He is with you always, even to the end of the age (Matthew 28:20).

Teaching them to observe all things that I have commanded you; and lo, I am with you always, even to the end of the age. Amen. Matthew 28:20

Living with Gratitude

Live with an attitude of gratitude, thanking God for His provision and faithfulness in all things. Cultivate a spirit of thankfulness for even the smallest blessings in your life, knowing that every good and perfect gift comes from above (James 1:17). Let your gratitude overflow into praise and worship, as you magnify the goodness and greatness of God.

For let not that man suppose that he will receive anything from the Lord; James 1:7

Prayer

Heavenly Father, thank you for your perfect peace and provision in my life. Help me to surrender fully to your sovereignty, trusting in your wisdom and goodness in all things. Grant me the grace to let go of anxiety and worry, and to trust in your unfailing provision for every need. May I rest in the assurance of your promises and abide in your presence, living with gratitude and praise for all you have done. In Jesus' name, amen.

Embracing Patience and Trust in Waiting Seasons

In life, we often find ourselves in waiting seasons, where things may not be progressing as quickly as we would like. During these times, it is important to embrace patience and trust in the process. Patience allows us to stay calm and composed, even when things seem uncertain or difficult. It enables us to have a positive outlook and believe that things will work out in the end. Trust, on the other hand, involves having faith in ourselves and the journey we are on. Trusting that everything is unfolding as it should, even if we cannot see the bigger picture at the moment, can bring a sense of peace and serenity.

Practicing patience and trust in waiting seasons can also lead to personal growth and self-discovery. It provides an opportunity for introspection and reflection, allowing us to reassess our goals, values, and priorities. By surrendering control and trusting the process, we can learn to let go of unnecessary worry and stress. It is a chance to cultivate resilience, adaptability, and a deeper sense of gratitude for the present moment. Embracing patience and trust in waiting seasons is not always easy, but it can lead to valuable insights and a renewed sense of hope for the future.

In this section, we will explore the transformative journey of embracing patience and trust during waiting seasons. By leaning on God's faithfulness and believing in His perfect timing, women can experience growth, strength, and deeper intimacy with Him as they wait expectantly for His plans to unfold.

Wait on the Lord; Be of good courage, And He shall strengthen your heart; Wait, I say, on the Lord! Psalms 27:14

Understanding the Purpose of Waiting

Begin by understanding the purpose of waiting seasons in your life. Recognize that waiting is not a passive activity but an opportunity for growth, refinement, and preparation. Trust that God is at work behind the scenes, orchestrating events according to His perfect timing and purposes. Be actively waiting by growing spiritual & emotional. Wait at the feet of Jesus and be of service to the Kingdom.

My brethren, count it all joy when you fall into various trials, knowing that the testing of your faith produces patience. But let patience have its perfect work, that you may be perfect and complete, lacking nothing. James 1:2-4

Cultivating Patience

Cultivate patience in the midst of waiting by trusting in God's timing and provision. Resist the urge to rush ahead or manipulate outcomes, and instead surrender yourself to His timing and will. Lean on His strength to endure the waiting process with grace and perseverance, knowing that He is faithful to sustain you.

Seeking God's Guidance

Seek God's guidance and direction during waiting seasons, through prayer, meditation on His Word, and seeking counsel from wise and godly mentors. Be attentive to His voice and leading, and follow wherever He may lead you, even if it means stepping into the unknown or enduring a period of uncertainty.

Finding Contentment in the Present

Find contentment and joy in the present moment, even as you wait for God's promises to be fulfilled. Choose to focus on the blessings and opportunities that surround you, rather than dwelling on what you lack or what you are waiting for. Trust that God has a purpose for every season of your life, and seek to glorify Him in all that you do.

Resting in God's Faithfulness

Rest in the faithfulness of God, knowing that He is true to His promises and His word never fails (Isaiah 55:11). Remind yourself of His past faithfulness in your life, and let it give you confidence and assurance as you wait for His plans to unfold. Trust that He who has begun a good work in you will carry it on to completion (Philippians 1:6).

Surrendering Control

Surrender control of your circumstances and outcomes to God, trusting that His ways are higher than yours and His thoughts are higher than yours (Isaiah 55:8-9). Release the need to understand or manipulate every aspect of your life, and instead entrust yourself fully into His loving care.

Rejoicing in Hope

Rejoice in hope, knowing that God is faithful to fulfill His promises in His perfect timing. Choose to praise Him in advance for what He is going to do, and let your heart be filled with joyful expectation and anticipation of His goodness. Rejoice in the Lord always, and again I say, rejoice (Philippians 4:4).

Rejoice in the Lord always. Again, I will say, rejoice! Philippians 4:4

Prayer

Heavenly Father, thank you for the opportunity to grow in patience and trust during waiting seasons. Help me to surrender control and find contentment in your perfect timing and provision. Grant me the grace to wait with joyful expectation and anticipation of your promises being fulfilled. May my waiting seasons be times of growth, strength, and deeper intimacy with you. In Jesus' name, amen.

Rejoicing in His Faithfulness and Promises

Rejoicing in the faithfulness and promises of a God can bring immense joy, comfort, and hope to individuals. Many people find solace in believing that there is a greater plan at work, and that they are being guided and supported by Holy Spirit. This faith can help individuals navigate through challenging times, providing them with a sense of peace and assurance that everything will work out in the end.

When we take the time to reflect on the faithfulness and promises of our beliefs, we are reminded of the unwavering support and love that surrounds us. This can inspire gratitude, positivity, and a sense of purpose in our lives. By focusing on the promises made by our faith, we can find strength and courage to face obstacles, knowing that we are not alone and that there is a greater power looking out for us.

In times of uncertainty or difficulty, turning to faith and meditating on the promises of God can bring clarity and peace to our hearts and minds. It is through this connection that we can find hope, resilience, and a deep sense of joy in knowing that we are never truly alone on our journey through life.

In this section, we will explore the joy and confidence that comes from rejoicing in God's faithfulness and promises. By anchoring our hearts in His unchanging character and word, women can experience a deep and lasting sense of joy, peace, and assurance in every season of life.

Reflecting on God's Faithfulness

Begin by reflecting on God's faithfulness in your life. Take time to remember the ways He has shown Himself faithful in the past, from the smallest blessings to the greatest miracles. Let these memories strengthen your faith and fill your heart with gratitude for His steadfast love and provision.

Therefore, know that the Lord your God, He is God, the faithful God who keeps covenant and mercy for a thousand generations with those who love Him and keep His commandments; Deuteronomy 7:9

Trusting in His Promises

Trust in the promises of God as anchors for your soul in times of uncertainty and doubt. Dive into His Word and discover the countless promises He has given to His children, promises of provision, protection, guidance, and eternal life. Choose to believe His promises, even when circumstances seem bleak, knowing that He who promised is faithful (Hebrews 10:23).

Rejoicing in His Character

Rejoice in the character of God, knowing that He is trustworthy, loving, and good. Celebrate His attributes of faithfulness, mercy, grace, and justice, and let them inspire confidence and hope in your heart. Rejoice that He is the same yesterday, today, and forever, and that His love endures forever (Psalm 136:1).

Therefore, as the elect of God, holy and beloved, put-on tender mercies, kindness, humility, meekness, longsuffering; Colossians 3:12

Praising Him in Advance

Praise God in advance for what He has promised to do, even before you see it come to fruition. Choose to praise Him for His faithfulness and goodness, regardless of your circumstances, and let your praise become a declaration of your faith and trust in Him. Rejoice that He is able to do immeasurably more than all we ask or imagine (Ephesians 3:20).

The voice of joy and the voice of gladness, the voice of the bridegroom and the voice of the bride, the voice of those who will say: "Praise the Lord of hosts, For the Lord is good, For His mercy endures forever"— and of those who will bring the sacrifice of praise into the house of the Lord. For I will cause the captives of the land to return as at the first," says the Lord. Jeremiah 33:11

Resting in His Sovereignty

Rest in the sovereignty of God, knowing that He is in control of all things and that His purposes will prevail. Surrender your desires and plans to His will, trusting that He is working all things together for your good and His glory (Romans 8:28). Find peace in knowing that His ways are higher than yours, and His thoughts are higher than yours (Isaiah 55:9).

Standing on His Word

Stand on the promises of God as you face challenges and trials in life. Let His Word be a lamp to your feet and a light to your path (Psalm 119:105), guiding you through every storm and valley. Declare His promises over your life with boldness and confidence, knowing that they are true and unchanging.

Your word is a lamp to my feet and a light to my path. Psalm 119:105

Step 7: Sharing His Faithfulness

Share the faithfulness of God with others, testifying to His goodness and grace in your life. Let your life be a living testimony to His faithfulness, and encourage others to trust in His promises and provision. Rejoice together in the faithfulness of our God, who is worthy of all praise and honor.

Prayer

Heavenly Father, thank you for your unchanging faithfulness and promises in my life. Help me to anchor my heart in your character and word, finding joy and confidence in your steadfast love and provision. Strengthen my faith as I reflect on your faithfulness in the past and trust in your promises for the future. May my life be a testimony to your goodness and grace, as I rejoice in your faithfulness and share it with others. In Jesus' name, amen.

Chapter 8: The Power of a Healed Woman

In this section, we will explore the transformative power of a healed woman. By experiencing healing in body, mind, and spirit, women can step into their full potential, impact their communities, and fulfill their God-given purposes with strength, grace, and authenticity.

Recognizing the Need for Healing

Begin by recognizing the need for healing in every area of your life. Acknowledge the wounds, hurts, and brokenness that you carry, whether they are physical, emotional, or spiritual. Understand that healing is a journey, and it starts with acknowledging the areas in need of restoration and surrendering them to God.

Seeking Healing from God

Seek healing from God, who is the ultimate healer of our bodies, minds, and spirits. Turn to Him in prayer, asking for His healing touch to restore you to wholeness and wellness. Trust in His power to heal every wound and mend every brokenness, believing that nothing is impossible for Him.

Embracing the Process of Healing

Embrace the process of healing with patience, perseverance, and faith. Understand that healing is not always immediate or linear, but it is a journey of growth, transformation, and renewal. Allow yourself to feel and process your emotions, and seek support from trusted friends, family, or professionals as needed.

Receiving God's Love and Forgiveness

Receive God's love and forgiveness as essential components of healing. Understand that God loves you unconditionally and desires to heal every part of you. Let go of guilt, shame, and condemnation, knowing that in Christ, you are forgiven and made new. Embrace His love and forgiveness, allowing them to wash over you and bring healing to your soul.

Extending Grace and Forgiveness to Yourself

Extend grace and forgiveness to yourself as you walk the path of healing. Release yourself from unrealistic expectations and self-criticism, and instead, offer yourself the same compassion and grace that God extends to you. Let go of past mistakes and failures, and embrace the freedom and joy that come from walking in forgiveness and grace.

Cultivating Wholeness in Every Area of Life

Cultivate wholeness in every area of your life – physically, emotionally, mentally, and spiritually. Prioritize self-care practices that nurture and restore you, such as exercise, healthy eating, rest, and relaxation. Invest in activities that bring you joy, fulfillment, and peace, and seek spiritual nourishment through prayer, worship, and fellowship with God.

Stepping into Your Purpose with Confidence

Step into your purpose with confidence and boldness, knowing that you are healed, whole, and empowered by God's grace. Embrace the unique gifts, talents, and passions that God has given you, and use them to make a positive impact in your community and beyond. Walk in the fullness of who God created you to be, shining brightly as a testimony to His healing power and love.

Prayer

Heavenly Father, thank you for your healing power that restores, renews, and transforms. I come to you in need of healing, surrendering every area of brokenness and woundedness into your loving hands. Heal me, Lord, in body, mind, and spirit, and make me whole and complete in you. Give me the strength, courage, and faith to embrace the journey of healing and step into my purpose with confidence and boldness. In Jesus' name, amen.

Embracing Wholeness in Christ

Discover the profound impact of embracing wholeness in Christ. As women experience healing in their relationship with God, they are liberated from shame, guilt, and condemnation, and empowered to live in the fullness of His love and grace.

In this section, we will explore the profound journey of embracing wholeness in Christ. By finding completeness and fulfillment in Him, women can experience true freedom, joy, and purpose in every aspect of their lives.

Understanding Wholeness in Christ

Begin by understanding what it means to find wholeness in Christ. Recognize that true wholeness comes from being rooted and grounded in Him, rather than in external circumstances or achievements. Understand that in Christ, you are complete and lacking nothing (Colossians 2:10), and that He alone can satisfy the deepest longings of your heart. The enemy has built foundations of lives going back to childhood abandonment from broken relations or lack thereof between parent and child. God is not like the parent that abandoned you. He is a good father. He will never harm you or leave you. The love we have learned from broken relationship is not the love or our father. His pure. His love cancels a multitude of sins. God wants to establish wholeness in Christ by His perfect design. The enemy plan is to keep you accustom to broken love, so you never recognize His love.

And you are complete in Him, who is the head of all principality and power.
Colossians 2:10

Surrendering to His Lordship

Surrender your life completely to the lordship of Christ, allowing Him to reign over every area of your life. Release control of your desires, plans, and ambitions, and submit yourself fully to His will and purposes. Trust in His wisdom and goodness, knowing that His plans for you are always good and perfect (Romans 12:2).

And do not be conformed to this world, but be transformed by the renewing of your mind, that you may prove what is that good and acceptable and perfect will of God.

Romans 12:2

Finding Identity in Him

Find your identity and worth in Christ alone, rather than in worldly pursuits or achievements. Understand that you are a beloved daughter of God, chosen, cherished, and accepted in Him (Ephesians 1:4-6). Let go of the need for validation or approval from others, and rest in the assurance of His love and acceptance. You are His beloved.

Just as He chose us in Him before the foundation of the world, that we should be holy and without blame before Him in love, having predestined us to adoption as sons by Jesus Christ to Himself, according to the good pleasure of His will, to the praise of the glory of His grace, by which He made us accepted in the Beloved. Ephesians 1:4-6

Receiving His Grace and Forgiveness

Receive His grace and forgiveness as essential components of wholeness. Understand that through His sacrifice on the cross, Jesus has paid the price for your sins and shortcomings, and His grace is more than sufficient to cover them all. Let go of guilt, shame, and condemnation, and embrace the freedom and joy that come from walking in forgiveness and grace.

Restoring Brokenness and Wounds

Allow Christ to restore and heal every area of brokenness and wounds in your life. Bring your hurts, pains, and struggles to Him in prayer, and allow His healing touch to bring restoration and renewal. Trust in His power to heal every wound and mend every brokenness, believing that nothing is impossible for Him.

Cultivating Intimacy with Him

Cultivate intimacy with Christ through prayer, worship, and fellowship with Him. Spend time in His presence daily, allowing His Spirit to minister to your heart and soul. Seek to know Him more deeply and intimately, and allow Him to reveal His love, grace, and truth to you in new and profound ways.

Walking in His Purpose

Walk in His purpose for your life with confidence and boldness, knowing that you are empowered by His Spirit to fulfill His calling. Surrender your gifts, talents, and passions to Him, and allow Him to use them for His glory and the benefit of others. Trust in His guidance and provision as you step out in faith to fulfill the purpose He has ordained for you.

Prayer

Heavenly Father, thank you for the gift of wholeness that we find in Christ alone. Help me to surrender my life completely to His lordship, finding my identity, worth, and fulfillment in Him alone. Heal every area of brokenness and wounds in my life, and restore me to wholeness and completeness in You. May I walk in intimacy with Christ, fulfilling His purpose for my life with confidence and boldness. In Jesus' name, amen.

Walking in Emotional Freedom

Explore the freedom that comes from healing emotional wounds and scars. As women confront past hurts, forgive those who have wronged them, and extend grace to themselves, they are liberated from the bondage of bitterness and resentment, and empowered to love and serve others with compassion.

In this section, we will explore the liberating journey of walking in emotional freedom. By addressing and overcoming emotional wounds, women can experience greater peace, joy, and resilience in their daily lives.

Acknowledging Emotional Wounds

Begin by acknowledging any emotional wounds or hurts that may be affecting your life. Recognize that it's okay to feel pain and that acknowledging these wounds is the first step toward healing. Be honest with yourself about the emotions you're experiencing and the areas in your life where you may need healing.

Seeking Healing and Restoration

Seek healing and restoration for your emotional wounds. Turn to God in prayer and ask Him to bring healing to the broken places in your heart. Seek out support from trusted friends, family members, or a counselor who can provide guidance and encouragement as you navigate this healing journey.

Letting Go of Past Hurts

Practice the art of forgiveness and let go of past hurts. Holding onto resentment and bitterness only serves to keep you trapped in emotional bondage. Choose to release these negative emotions and extend forgiveness to those who have wronged you, whether they ask for it or not. Remember that forgiveness is a gift you give yourself, freeing you from the weight of carrying grudges.

Embracing Vulnerability and Authenticity

Embrace vulnerability and authenticity in your relationships. Allow yourself to be seen and known for who you truly are, flaws and all. Share your struggles and triumphs with others, knowing that true connection and healing come from being open and honest about your experiences.

Practicing Self-Compassion

Practice self-compassion and kindness toward yourself. Treat yourself with the same love and understanding that you would offer to a dear friend who is struggling. Be gentle with yourself during times of difficulty and remind yourself that you are worthy of love and acceptance just as you are.

Cultivating Healthy Coping Mechanisms

Cultivate healthy coping mechanisms for managing stress and difficult emotions. Engage in activities that bring you joy and relaxation, such as exercise, hobbies, or spending time in nature. Develop a support network of friends and loved ones who can offer encouragement and companionship during challenging times.

Walking in Freedom and Wholeness

Finally, commit to walking in freedom and wholeness each day. Choose to let go of the past and embrace the present moment with gratitude and optimism. Trust that God is working all things together for your good and that He has a beautiful plan for your life. Walk confidently in the knowledge that you are loved, valued, and cherished by your Heavenly Father.

Prayer

Heavenly Father, I thank you for the gift of emotional freedom that you offer to each of us. I pray that you would bring healing and restoration to any emotional wounds that I may be carrying. Help me to let go of past hurts and embrace vulnerability and authenticity in my relationships. Grant me the strength to practice self-compassion and cultivate healthy coping mechanisms. May I walk in freedom and wholeness each day, trusting in your unfailing love and grace. In Jesus' name, amen.

Renewing the Mind

Understand the importance of renewing the mind with God's truth. As women replace negative thought patterns with the truth of Scripture, they are transformed from the inside out, experiencing greater peace, joy, and confidence in their identity as daughters of the King.

In this section, we will delve into the transformative process of renewing the mind. By intentionally shaping our thoughts and beliefs according to God's truth, women can experience profound personal growth, spiritual maturity, and lasting change in their lives.

Recognizing the Power of the Mind

Begin by recognizing the power of the mind to shape your reality. Your thoughts and beliefs influence your emotions, actions, and ultimately, your destiny. Understand that renewing your mind is a vital component of spiritual growth and personal transformation.

Identifying Negative Thought Patterns

Identify negative thought patterns that may be hindering your growth and well-being. These could include self-doubt, fear, worry, or toxic beliefs about yourself, others, or God. Take inventory of your thought life and recognize patterns that do not align with God's truth and love.

Aligning with Biblical Truth

Align your thoughts and beliefs with biblical truth. Spend time in God's Word daily, allowing it to shape your thinking and renew your mind. Replace negative thought patterns with God's promises, affirmations of faith, and truths about your identity in Christ.

Practicing Mindfulness and Awareness

Practice mindfulness and awareness of your thoughts throughout the day. Pay attention to the thoughts that enter your mind and evaluate them against God's Word. Choose to reject thoughts that are contrary to His truth and replace them with thoughts that are pure, noble, and uplifting (Philippians 4:8).

Guarding Your Mind & Heart

Guard your mind against negative influences and distractions that can lead you away from God's truth. Be discerning about the media you consume, the conversations you engage in, and the environments you expose yourself to. Surround yourself with positive influences that encourage and support your spiritual growth.

And the peace of God, which surpasses all understanding, will guard your hearts and minds through Christ Jesus. Philippians 4:7

Renewing Your Thought Life Daily

Make renewing your mind a daily practice. Set aside time each day for prayer, meditation on scriptures, and reflection. Invite the Holy Spirit to renew your mind and transform your thinking according to God's will.

Cultivating Gratitude and Positivity

Cultivate an attitude of gratitude and positivity in your thought life. Focus on the blessings in your life and the goodness of God, even in the midst of challenges. Choose to see the world through the lens of faith and hope, trusting in God's faithfulness and sovereignty.

Prayer

Heavenly Father, I thank you for the gift of a renewed mind that comes through your Word and Spirit. Help me to identify and replace negative thought patterns with your truth and love. Renew my mind daily according to your will, that I may grow in spiritual maturity and experience lasting transformation. May my thoughts be pleasing to you, and may they lead me closer to your heart. In Jesus' name, amen.

Embracing Purpose and Calling

Discover the significance of embracing purpose and calling. As women surrender their lives to God's plan and follow His leading, they are empowered to step into their God-given destiny, using their gifts and talents to make a difference in the world around them.

In this section, we will explore the empowering journey of embracing purpose and calling. By discovering and walking in alignment with God's unique plan for their lives, women can experience fulfillment, impact, and joy beyond measure.

Seeking God's Guidance

Begin by seeking God's guidance in discovering your purpose and calling. Spend time in prayer, asking Him to reveal His plan for your life and to clarify the gifts, talents, and passions He has given you. Trust that He will guide you as you seek His will with an open heart.

Reflecting on Your Gifts and Passions

Reflect on your gifts, talents, and passions as clues to your purpose and calling. Consider the activities and endeavors that bring you the greatest joy and fulfillment, as well as the areas where others affirm your strengths and abilities. Pay attention to recurring themes or interests that resonate deeply with your heart.

Listening to God's Voice

Listen to God's voice through His Word, prayer, and the promptings of His Spirit. Be open to His leading and guidance, even if it takes you out of your comfort zone or challenges your preconceived notions. Trust that He knows you intimately and has a perfect plan for your life.

Stepping Out in Faith

Step out in faith as you discern and pursue your purpose and calling. Trust that God will equip you with everything you need to fulfill His plan for your life (Hebrews 13:21), and be willing to take risks and follow His leading, even when it seems daunting or uncertain.

Make you complete in every good work to do His will, working in you what is well pleasing in His sight, through Jesus Christ, to whom be glory forever and ever. Amen. Hebrews 13:21

Embracing Your Unique Contribution

Embrace your unique contribution to God's kingdom and the world around you. Recognize that you have been created with a specific purpose and calling, and that your gifts and talents are valuable tools for advancing His kingdom. Celebrate your individuality and the ways in which God desires to use you to make a difference.

Serving Others with Love

Serve others with love and compassion as you walk in alignment with your purpose and calling. Look for opportunities to use your gifts and talents to bless and uplift those around you, whether it's through acts of kindness, words of encouragement, or sharing the love of Christ in practical ways.

Remaining Flexible and Open

Remain flexible and open to God's leading as you journey along the path of purpose and calling. Understand that His plans may unfold in unexpected ways, and be willing to adapt and adjust as He directs your steps. Trust that He is faithful to guide you every step of the way.

Prayer

Heavenly Father, I thank you for the unique purpose and calling you have placed on my life. Guide me in discovering and embracing your plan for me, and give me the courage and faith to step out in obedience. Help me to serve others with love and compassion, and to remain flexible and open to your leading. May my life be a reflection of your glory and a testimony to your goodness. In Jesus' name, amen.

Impacting Generations

Recognize the ripple effect of a healed woman's life. As women experience healing and restoration, they become agents of change in their families, communities, and beyond, impacting future generations for the glory of God.

In this section, we will explore the profound opportunity and responsibility of impacting generations. By living intentionally and investing in the lives of others, women can leave a lasting legacy that extends far beyond their own lifetime.

Embracing the Power of Influence

Begin by embracing the power of your influence to impact generations. Recognize that your words, actions, and choices have the potential to shape the lives of those around you, both now and in the future. Understand that even small acts of kindness and love can have ripple effects that span generations.

Investing in Relationships

Invest in relationships with intentionality and purpose. Take the time to nurture and strengthen your relationships with family members, friends, mentors, and mentees. Be present and engaged in the lives of those around you, offering support, encouragement, and wisdom as needed.

Modeling Faith and Integrity

Model faith and integrity in all areas of your life. Let your words and actions align with your beliefs, demonstrating the transformative power of a life lived in obedience to God's Word. Be a beacon of light and hope to those around you, inspiring others to walk in faith and righteousness.

Sharing Your Story

Share your story and experiences with humility and vulnerability. Be willing to open up about the challenges you've faced, the lessons you've learned, and the faithfulness of God in your life. Your testimony has the power to inspire and encourage others, helping them to navigate their own journey with hope and perseverance.

And they overcame him by the blood of the Lamb and by the word of their testimony, and they did not love their lives to the death. Revelations 12:11

Mentoring and Discipling

Mentor and disciple, the next generation of leaders and influencers. Look for opportunities to invest in the lives of younger women, sharing your wisdom, knowledge, and experiences with them. Be a source of guidance and support as they navigate life's challenges and pursue their God-given dreams and ambitions.

Leaving a Legacy of Love

Leave a legacy of love that will endure for generations to come. Seek to leave behind a lasting impact on the lives of those you encounter, showing kindness, compassion, and grace to all. Live with eternity in mind, knowing that the investments you make in the lives of others have eternal significance.

Trusting God with the Outcome

Finally, trust God with the outcome of your efforts to impact generations. Understand that ultimately, He is the one who brings about lasting change and transformation in the hearts and lives of people. Surrender your desires and plans to Him, trusting that He will use your obedience and faithfulness for His glory and purposes.

Prayer

Heavenly Father, thank you for the privilege and responsibility of impacting generations. Help me to steward my influence with wisdom and grace, that I may leave a lasting legacy of love and faithfulness. Guide me in investing in relationships, modeling faith and integrity, sharing my story, and mentoring the next generation. May my life bring glory to your name and lead others into a deeper relationship with you. In Jesus' name, amen.

Continuing in Faith

Commit to continuing in faith on the journey of healing and restoration. As women persevere through trials and challenges, they are strengthened by God's grace and equipped to overcome every obstacle that stands in their way.

The importance of continuing in faith, even in the face of challenges, doubts, and uncertainties. By steadfastly trusting in God's promises and faithfulness, women can persevere through trials and experience the fullness of His blessings and provision.

Remembering God's Faithfulness

Begin by remembering God's faithfulness in your life and throughout history. Reflect on the times when He has come through for you, provided for you, and answered your prayers. Let these memories strengthen your faith and serve as a reminder of His steadfast love and faithfulness.

Anchoring Yourself in His Word

Anchor yourself in God's Word as the foundation of your faith. Spend time daily reading and meditating on Scripture, allowing it to nourish and sustain your soul. Let His promises and truths be a source of strength and encouragement, guiding you through every season of life.

Praying Without Ceasing

Pray without ceasing, maintaining a constant and intimate connection with God. Share your hopes, fears, dreams, and struggles with Him in prayer, knowing that He hears and cares for you deeply.

Trust in His ability to answer your prayers according to His perfect will and timing.

Seeking His Will

Seek God's will for your life with humility and surrender. Trust that His plans are always good and perfect, even when they may not align with your own desires or expectations. Surrender your plans and ambitions to Him, allowing His Spirit to guide you in the paths of righteousness.

Walking in Obedience

Walk in obedience to God's commands and promptings, even when it requires sacrifice or stepping out of your comfort zone. Trust that obedience is the pathway to blessing and fulfillment, and that God rewards those who diligently seek Him (Hebrews 11:6).

Finding Strength in Community

Find strength and encouragement in the community of believers. Surround yourself with fellow Christians who can offer support, prayer, and accountability as you continue in faith. Share your burdens and joys with one another, knowing that you are not alone in your journey.

Persevering with Hope

Persevere with hope, knowing that God is faithful to complete the work He has begun in you (Philippians 1:6). Even in the midst of trials and tribulations, hold fast to the hope of eternity and the promise of His return. Trust that He is able to do immeasurably more than all we ask or imagine (Ephesians 3:20).

Being confident of this very thing, that He who has begun a good work in you will complete it until the day of Jesus Christ;

Philippians 1:6

Prayer

Heavenly Father, thank you for the gift of faith that sustains us through every trial and challenge. Help me to continue in faith, anchoring myself in your Word, praying without ceasing, seeking your will, walking in obedience, finding strength in community, and persevering with hope. Strengthen my faith, Lord, that I may trust in your promises and experience the fullness of your blessings. Thank you for the transformative power of healing and restoration in Christ. Empower me to walk in wholeness, emotional freedom, and purpose, impacting the world around me for your glory. May my life be a testimony to your goodness and grace. In Jesus' name, amen.

Conclusion: The Power of a Healed Woman

In the journey of "Healing Grace: The Power of a Healed Woman," we've explored the transformative process of healing, renewal, and empowerment that comes from embracing God's grace and walking in His truth. From acknowledging pain and brokenness to embracing purpose and calling, each chapter has offered guidance, encouragement, and practical steps for women to experience wholeness, freedom, and fulfillment in Christ.

As we conclude this journey, let us reflect on the profound truth that God's healing grace is available to each of us, no matter our past hurts or present struggles. He is the ultimate healer who can restore every broken piece of our lives and transform us into vessels of His love and grace.

Take Away:

- **You are Loved:** Remember that you are deeply loved and cherished by your Heavenly Father. His love knows no bounds and His grace is more than sufficient for every need you may have.
- **You are Valued:** Recognize your inherent worth and value as a daughter of the Most High God. You are fearfully and wonderfully made, with unique gifts, talents, and purposes ordained by God Himself.
- **You are Empowered:** Understand that you are empowered by the Holy Spirit to overcome every obstacle and walk in victory. Through Christ, you have the strength, courage, and resilience to face whatever challenges may come your way.
- **You are Called:** Embrace your calling and purpose in Christ, knowing that you have been chosen and appointed for such a

time as this. God has a specific plan and destiny for your life, and He will equip you with everything you need to fulfill it.

- **You are Not Alone:** Finally, remember that you are not alone on this journey. God is with you every step of the way, guiding, comforting, and empowering you to become the woman He created you to be. Surround yourself with a community of believers who can offer support, encouragement, and accountability as you continue to grow in your relationship with Jesus.

As you move forward from this journey, may you be encouraged, edified, impacted, and changed by the truth of God's Word and the power of His healing grace. May you continue to grow in your relationship with Jesus, walking in faith, freedom, and purpose each day. And may you shine brightly as a beacon of His love and grace to a world in need of healing and hope. My pray for you is that nothing can keep you away from the love of God.

With love and blessings,

Genea' Waller

FAITH CONFESSION OF A HEALED WOMAN

In the name of Jesus, I declare:

I am a healed woman, redeemed by the blood of the Lamb. By His wounds, I am made whole, body, mind, and spirit.

I confess that God's healing grace flows through me, restoring every broken place and bringing renewal to every area of my life.

I am no longer defined by my past hurts or present struggles. I am a new creation in Christ, empowered by His Spirit to walk in victory and freedom.

HEALING GRACE: THE POWER OF A HEALED WOMAN

I declare that I am loved with an everlasting love, cherished and valued by my Heavenly Father. His love surrounds me, sustains me, and gives me the strength to overcome.

I reject every lie of the enemy that seeks to steal my joy, kill my faith, and destroy my confidence. I am more than a conqueror through Christ who strengthens me.

I confess that I am called and chosen for a purpose greater than myself. God has a plan and destiny for my life, and I walk boldly in obedience to His will.

I release forgiveness to those who have wronged me, letting go of bitterness, resentment, and unforgiveness. I am free to love and forgive as Christ has loved and forgiven me.

I declare that I am a vessel of God's healing grace, bringing hope, restoration, and transformation wherever I go. I shine brightly as a light in the darkness, pointing others to the love and power of Jesus Christ.

I am filled with faith, hope, and expectation for the miraculous. I believe in the power of prayer to bring about healing, breakthrough, and miracles in my life and the lives of those around me.

I declare these truths in faith, knowing that God is faithful to fulfill His promises and bring His purposes to pass in my life. I walk in confidence, knowing that I am a healed woman, empowered to live victoriously for the glory of God. Amen.

I love you, Healed Woman

Don't miss out!

Visit the website below and you can sign up to receive emails whenever Genea' Waller publishes a new book. There's no charge and no obligation.

https://books2read.com/r/B-A-BPIEB-RCLYC

BOOKS 2 READ

Connecting independent readers to independent writers.

About the Author

Genea' Waller is a multifaceted individual, embodying the roles of prophet, teacher, intercessor, entrepreneur, change agent, and visionary. Raised in the vibrant city of Houston, Texas, Genea' Waller's journey has been one of spiritual discovery, growth, and obedience to the call of God on her life.

From a young age, Genea' demonstrated a deep sensitivity to the voice of God and a profound understanding of spiritual truths. Her upbringing by a single mother who was supportive and provided a solid foundation for her faith, while her experiences navigating the challenges of life in Houston helped shape her into the resilient and determined individual she is today.

Answering the call of God on her life as a prophet of the Lord, Genea' Waller embarked on a journey of faith and obedience, allowing God to mold and shape her into His vessel of change and transformation. With a heart for intercession and a passion for seeing God's kingdom established on earth, Genea' has dedicated her life to proclaiming God's truth, teaching His word, and mobilizing others to pray and intercede for revival and awakening.

In addition to her ministry calling, Genea' Waller is also a successful entrepreneur, using her business acumen and visionary leadership to impact her community and beyond. Her innovative spirit and commitment to excellence have led her to create and steward various initiatives and enterprises aimed at bringing about positive change and empowering others to reach their full potential.

As a change agent and visionary, Genea' Waller is committed to pushing the boundaries of what is possible and inspiring others to dream big and pursue their God-given destiny. Whether through her prophetic insights, teaching ministry, entrepreneurial endeavors, or acts of service, Genea' continues to leave a lasting impact on those around her, igniting hearts and minds with the fire of God's love and truth.

Genea' Waller's life and ministry are a testament to the transformative power of faith, obedience, and surrender to God's will. With unwavering determination and a heart ablaze with passion for God's kingdom, she continues to press forward, leaving a trail of hope, inspiration, and transformation in her wake.

www.ingramcontent.com/pod-product-compliance
Lightning Source LLC
Chambersburg PA
CBHW072240150726
48002CB00005B/2174